I0093182

Find more of my work at my blog:

www.theauthorstack.com

Find all my work at my website:

www.russellnohelty.com

Bookbub:

https://www.bookbub.com/profile/russell-nohelty

DIRECT SALES STRATEGY FOR AUTHORS

By:
Russell Nohelty

Edited by:
Lily Luchesi

Proofread by:
Katrina Roets

Copyright © 2025 by Russell Nohelty

Published by Wannabe Press

All Rights Reserved.

This is a nonfiction work. Russell Nohelty and Wannabe Press do not guarantee any outcomes from following the advice in this book. We are not lawyers, accountants, or other specialized professionals. We take no responsibility for what happens if you take this advice. It's worked for us and many others we know. However, this is simply the accumulated experience of one man making his journey into the world. While we think it is very good advice, there is no guarantee it will work for you.

First Edition, August 2025

THIS IS THE WORK THAT WORKS

Direct sales is the throughline of my career. It's not something I pivoted to after things fell apart elsewhere. It's what made the whole thing possible in the first place.

I've sold tens of thousands of books directly through Kickstarter, my webstore, live events, and more. I've raised millions of dollars for my own creative projects, and I've helped hundreds of other authors do the same.

So this isn't a theory book. It's not a trend book. This is the culmination of *doing the work*—figuring out what sells, what flops, and what actually builds long-term, meaningful success without burning out in the process.

If you're tired of giving 70% of your earnings to platforms that won't even show your book to your followers... welcome. You're my kind of person.

I've spent the last twenty years building a creative career across nearly every medium you can think of, including fiction, comics, nonfiction, film, audio, games, education, and more. I've launched books, sold out conventions, raised hundreds of thousands of dollars for my projects, licensed my work to board game companies and coffee brands, and gotten optioned by studios. I've been repped by litcrary agents and managers, worked with A-list showrunners, and pitched to companies like Nickelodeon and Disney.

I've had book signings on multiple continents. Sold books into translation. Created courses. Directed TV. Designed websites. Built tools. Sat on boards. Spoken to audiences around the world. And yeah, I've flamed out, too. I've had launches fail, partnerships break, and ideas that just didn't work. That's part of the deal.

But I don't see myself as someone who just "writes books." I build systems. I test markets. I look at author careers like real businesses, because that's what they are, and how we should treat them.

That's the lens I bring to this work, because writing is magic, but you still have to pay the soup man. You're literally creating hallucinations in someone else's brain and making them feel something real. But turning that into a *business*? That takes more than magic. That takes intention. Structure. Skill.

That's what this book, and all my work, is here to help you do.

I believe there is a way forward for every author. Not just the lucky ones. Not just the bestselling ones. Everyone.

You don't need to chase every trend. You don't need to go viral. You just need a system that fits your goals, your audience, and your life. That's what I've built for myself, and what I help others build every day.

So, if you're tired of guessing and ready to take real control of your creative future, you're in the right place.

This book is everything I've learned about direct sales after launching over a dozen successful Kickstarters, running hundreds of live events, and building a webstore that people actually buy from.

The publishing world doesn't make it easy to learn this stuff. Most authors are trained to think that Amazon is the only way to sell books. That if you're not ranking on some algorithm, you're invisible. That "marketing" means running an ad, hoping for clicks, and burning out before you make a hundred bucks.

That's not a business. That's a slot machine.

I don't want to teach you how to chase luck. I want to show you how to build a system. A repeatable, ethical, creative system that brings readers in, keeps them engaged, and lets you sell without selling your soul.

Direct sales isn't just about making more money per book (though you probably will). It's about control, flexibility, and ownership. It's about building something you can actually grow without begging for permission from a platform that doesn't care if you succeed.

But none of this happens by accident. You need structure. You need strategy. And that's what this book delivers.

We'll cover:

- How to build a homepage and store that actually convert
- What makes landing pages work (and why most don't)
- How to sell confidently at live events
- How to run a Kickstarter like a launch, not a hope
- How to pace, bundle, and position your work so it sells

This isn't a theory. It's based on what I've done, what's failed, and what's worked well enough to do again. So, if you're ready to stop chasing scraps and start building something real, let's go.

UNDERSTANDING THE MODERN CUSTOMER JOURNEY

The art of turning a stranger into a loyal customer has never been more complex or more important than in today's digital landscape. Making that transition might not be a subconscious decision on the customer's part, but that customer journey should very much be front of mind as we plot out our sales process.

A customer journey represents every interaction someone has with your brand, from their first glimpse of your content to the moment they become a devoted repeat customer and beyond.

Think of it like a first date that blossoms into a long-term relationship. Just as you wouldn't propose marriage at first sight, you shouldn't expect an immediate purchase from someone who's just discovered your brand. Instead, the journey unfolds through carefully orchestrated touchpoints, each one building upon the last to create a deeper connection.

Creators who truly grasp this concept don't just see isolated interactions. Instead, they see a continuous story unfolding. Every email opened, every social media post liked, and every website visit becomes a chapter in your customer's unique narrative with your brand.

Success lies not in perfecting any single touchpoint, but in weaving them together into a coherent, compelling experience that naturally guides customers toward a lasting relationship with your brand.

Traditional marketing wisdom breaks down the customer's path into distinct stages — awareness, consideration, and decision — but modern digital tools have transformed this simple progression into something far more dynamic. Today's marketers can accelerate and enhance each stage of this journey through strategic content, targeted messaging, and perfectly timed touchpoints.

What makes contemporary marketing particularly powerful is its ability to meet customers exactly where they are in their journey. *A well-crafted strategy can transform complete strangers into interested prospects, nurture those prospects into engaged followers, and convert those followers into passionate customers who not only buy but advocate for your brand.*

Gone are the days when marketing meant shouting your message into the void, hoping the right people would hear it. Modern digital tools allow us to create personalized experiences that respond to each customer's unique needs and interests. This precision in targeting and messaging means every interaction can be more meaningful, more relevant, and ultimately more effective at moving customers along their journey.

ANATOMY OF A CUSTOMER JOURNEY

To truly understand how customer journeys work in practice, let's follow a potential customer we'll call Bob. Bob is digitally savvy, but also selective about where he spends both his time and money. He's experienced enough with online marketing to be skeptical of obvious sales pitches, yet he's open to authentic connections with brands that align with his interests.

One evening, while unwinding after work, Bob comes across a piece of content that catches his eye. It's a thoughtfully designed giveaway for collectors of vintage sci-fi memorabilia, one of his passionate interests that he rarely indulges. The timing is perfect; he's just finished reorganizing his collection and has been thinking about expanding it. ***This isn't just any promotional content, though.*** It's been carefully crafted to appeal to true enthusiasts, with prizes that demonstrate a real understanding of the community.

The initial touchpoint is the beginning of Bob's journey. After clicking through, he arrives at a landing page that speaks his language, featuring references that only true fans would appreciate. The page isn't just pimping an offer to buy. It's filled with interesting content about collecting, preservation tips, and stories from other collectors. So, he signs up to the company's promotional material, what we call an "opt-in."

When he finally signs up to learn more, the experience is seamless. Instead of an abrupt "thanks for entering" message, he receives a personalized email that includes a curated guide to caring for vintage collectibles, something of genuine value whether he buys from the company or not. The brand has ***anticipated his needs and interests***, providing relevant content before he even asks for it.

How can they do that? Because they've spent a lot of time talking to people just like Bob and know what they want, so they speak the same shared language Bob knows, endearing themselves to him almost immediately.

Over the next few weeks, Bob's journey continues to unfold naturally. He receives carefully timed follow-up emails, each containing valuable content rather than just promotional messages. There's an introduction to an online community of fellow collectors, exclusive interviews with notable figures in the vintage sci-fi world, and behind-the-scenes looks at rare collections. Bob finds himself increasingly engaged with the brand's content.

What makes this journey particularly effective is its organic progression. ***The brand doesn't push for a sale immediately.*** Instead, they demonstrate their expertise and value through consistently helpful content and genuine community engagement. When they do eventually present Bob with an offer—an exclusive pre-sale for a limited-edition piece—it feels less like a sales pitch and more like a natural extension of the relationship they've built.

This journey showcases several crucial elements of effective customer journey design:

1. The ***initial hook*** is precisely targeted to Bob's interests and presented at a moment when he's most receptive.
2. Each ***touchpoint*** builds upon the previous one, creating a coherent narrative rather than disconnected interactions.
3. ***Value*** is provided consistently, not just when trying to make a sale.
4. The relationship is ***nurtured*** through relevant content and community engagement.
5. The eventual ***sales offer*** is presented in context as part of an ongoing relationship rather than a cold pitch.

By the time Bob makes his first purchase, he's not just buying a product. He's deepening his engagement with a brand that has already provided significant value. This is the essence of a well-designed customer journey: it transforms what could have been a simple transaction into a meaningful relationship that benefits both the customer and the brand, which is why authors need to think of themselves as one.

DIFFERENT TYPES OF CUSTOMER JOURNEYS

While Bob's journey into the world of vintage collectibles illustrates one path, customer journeys are as diverse as businesses themselves. Each industry, product type, and business model demands its own unique approach to guiding customers from discovery to purchase and beyond.

While we've explored the basic framework of customer journeys, let's focus on what this means specifically for authors. The path a reader takes from discovering your book to becoming a devoted fan has its own unique characteristics and opportunities.

Consider the journey of someone discovering a new author. It might begin with a recommendation from a friend or a striking book cover that catches their eye while browsing online. They read the sample chapters, intrigued by the writing style.

Rather than immediately purchasing the book, they might follow the author on social media, discovering their background and the stories behind their stories. They sign up for the author's newsletter, receive updates about the writing process, and feel increasingly connected to the author's world. When they finally purchase and read the book, it's not just a transaction. It's the latest chapter in an ongoing relationship. This connection often leads them to eagerly await the next release, participate in book discussions, and recommend the author to other readers.

Let's now look at the journey of discovering a new favorite author. It often begins in unexpected places like a friend's enthusiastic recommendation, an intriguing review on Goodreads, or a captivating social media post about your book's theme. The potential reader might then peek at your author website, where they find not just book information, but glimpses into your writing process through blog posts or behind-the-scenes content.

The beauty of an author's customer journey lies in its emotional depth. Reading a book is an intimate experience, quite different from purchasing a typical product. Your readers aren't just buying pages bound together. They're investing hours of their time in the world you've created. This journey often starts with small commitments: following you on social media, signing up for your newsletter, or downloading a free short story. Each of these touchpoints helps build trust and familiarity with your voice as a writer.

What makes author journeys particularly special is their cyclical nature. Unlike many products where the customer journey ends with a purchase, book readers often become more invested after finishing your book. They join your reader groups, participate in book discussions, eagerly await your next release, and become advocates who recommend your work to others. Many readers actually strengthen their connection to an author between books, through interactions with your content, your community, and other readers who share their enthusiasm.

Take the example of a thriller author who understands this journey. They might start by sharing intriguing true crime stories that inspired their writing on social media, drawing in readers who share this interest.

Their newsletter might offer exclusive short stories featuring side characters from their books, keeping readers engaged between releases. They could host virtual book clubs where readers discuss not just the plot, but the deeper themes and research behind the story. Each of these touchpoints deepens the readers' connection to both the author's work and their creative world.

This deeper understanding of the readers' journey helps authors move beyond simply promoting their latest release. *Instead, they can create an ongoing relationship with readers that enriches both sides of the equation.* The goal isn't just to sell one book, it's to create a lasting connection that turns first-time readers into lifelong fans.

THE HIDDEN DEPTH OF CUSTOMER JOURNEYS

Today's customers rarely follow a straight path to purchase. They might discover your brand through a social media post, then encounter your newsletter content, while simultaneously seeing your products reviewed by their favorite influencer.

Each of these touchpoints creates a unique impression, contributing to their overall perception of your brand. It's less like a funnel and more like a constellation of connected experiences.

What makes this even more complex is the way customers move between stages. Someone might be deeply familiar with your brand but return to the research phase when considering a new product line. A loyal customer might suddenly need reassurance about their choice when a competitor launches a new offering. ***These movements aren't failures of the journey, but natural patterns of human decision-making that smart brands learn to anticipate and support.***

Consider how a customer might interact with a premium skincare brand. They might first encounter the brand through a friend's recommendation, then read reviews while simultaneously following the brand's educational content about skin health. They might add products to their cart, abandon them, return to read more about ingredients, watch user testimonials, and finally make a purchase, only to start a similar journey when considering their next product. ***Each of these micro-journeys contains valuable information about customer needs, hesitations, and motivations.***

The depth of customer journeys extends beyond just purchasing decisions. Every interaction leaves an emotional impression that influences future engagement. A particularly helpful customer service interaction might turn a one-time buyer into a brand advocate. A thoughtful follow-up email might transform a casual browser into a loyal customer. These emotional touchpoints often prove more valuable than traditional marketing metrics would suggest.

Digital technology has made these complex journeys both more possible and more visible. Customers expect brands to remember their preferences, anticipate their needs, and provide relevant information at exactly the right moment. Yet they also want these personalized experiences to feel natural and unobtrusive. This delicate balance requires understanding not just where customers are in their journey, but also why they're there and what might help them move forward.

The true complexity of customer journeys often reveals itself in the unusual patterns that emerge from data. One customer might engage with your high-end products for months before making their first purchase. Another might bounce between your educational content and competitor comparisons for weeks, only to become one of your most valuable customers. These patterns remind us that customer journeys are fundamentally human stories, full of the same contradictions and complexities that characterize all human decision-making.

LEARNING FROM SUCCESS STORIES

Success leaves clues, and in the publishing world, examining how successful authors build their readership offers invaluable insights into effective reader journeys. By studying these success stories, we can uncover patterns that work specifically in the book market, regardless of genre or style.

Take the approach of V.E. Schwab, who has masterfully built her readership through genuine connection. Beyond her compelling stories, she shares her writing struggles and triumphs openly on social media, creating a sense of shared journey with her readers. Her transparency about the creative process, combined with her engagement with fan art and reader discussions, shows how authenticity can transform readers into a passionate community.

Or consider how Leigh Bardugo has expanded her reader relationships beyond individual books. She doesn't just publish stories; she creates an immersive experience around the Grishaverse. Through thoughtful world-building content, engaging with fan theories, and creating supplementary materials that enrich her world, she transforms readers from casual observers into invested participants in an ever-expanding universe.

Romance authors often excel at reader journey design. Authors like Talia Hibbert have built devoted followings by creating vibrant reader communities. She understands her books aren't just standalone products but gateways to a shared experience. Through engaging social media presence, thoughtful discussion of romance tropes, and open conversations about representation in literature, she's created a space where readers feel both seen and valued.

The most successful authors understand that value must be delivered beyond the books themselves. Whether it's through thoughtful book club questions, engaging social media presence, or newsletter content that entertains as well as informs, these authors excel at creating what feels like a natural progression of engagement with their readers.

Consider how thriller author Lucy Foley builds her reader relationships. She doesn't just promote her next release. She creates carefully structured pathways that guide readers deeper into her world of mysteries. Through sharing her research process, discussing the real-world locations that inspire her settings, and engaging with readers' theories, she keeps her community engaged between books and creates multiple entry points for new readers.

Perhaps the most valuable lesson from successful authors is their ability to turn transactional relationships into emotional connections. They understand that while an intriguing plot might initially attract readers, it's the emotional resonance of the entire experience that creates lasting loyalty.

Whether it's through personal notes to readers, sharing the challenges of the writing process, or creating special moments for their community, these connections transform ordinary reader relationships into meaningful, long-term engagement.

PLOTTING YOUR READER JOURNEY

The concept of customer journeys might sound great in theory, but how do you actually create one for your readers? Let's break down the practical steps of mapping out your reader's path from discovery to superfan.

Start with the end in mind. What do you want your ideal reader relationship to look like? Perhaps it's a devoted fan who pre-orders every book, engages in your reader community, and recommends your work to others. Or maybe it's someone who subscribes to your premium content tier and attends your virtual events. This vision becomes your journey's destination.

Now, work backwards. If we imagine your reader's experience as a series of stepping stones, each one should be a small, achievable commitment that naturally leads to the next. For example:

First Encounter → Content Sampling → First Purchase → Community Engagement → Loyal Reader → Active Advocate

For each of these stages, you'll need *three key elements*: a way for readers to find that stepping stone, clear value that makes them want to step on it, and an obvious path to the next stone. Let's break this down practically:

First Encounter might happen through social media posts about your book's theme, blog posts that showcase your writing style, or newsletter swaps with similar authors. The key is making this first touch point intriguing enough for readers to want more.

Content Sampling could be the first few chapters available on your website, a free prequel novella, or exclusive short stories. This gives readers a risk-free way to experience your writing and connect with your style.

The path to *First Purchase* needs to be crystal clear. Your sample content should lead naturally to information about your full books, with easy links to purchase. Consider offering a special incentive for newsletter subscribers, like bonus epilogues or character interviews.

Community Engagement might start small – encouraging readers to follow your social media or join your reader group. Make sure you're offering value here too, whether it's behind-the-scenes content, early cover reveals, or simple engagement with fellow fans.

The transition to *Loyal Reader* often happens through consistent delivery of both books and supplementary content. This might include exclusive newsletter content, special editions for subscribers, or early access to new releases.

Finally, *Active Advocates* emerge when you make it easy and rewarding to spread the word about your books. This could be through shareable content, referral rewards, or simply by creating such a compelling experience that readers naturally want to tell others.

Remember to install feedback mechanisms at each stage. Analytics tools, reader surveys, and direct conversations with your audience can help you understand where readers might be getting stuck or losing interest in their journey.

Most importantly, *be patient.* Building these pathways takes time, and it's okay to start small. Focus on creating one clear path first, then expand and refine it based on what you learn from your readers' behavior and feedback.

THE FUTURE OF CUSTOMER JOURNEYS

As we look toward the horizon of customer experience, the evolution of customer journeys is accelerating at an unprecedented pace. Artificial intelligence and machine learning are transforming what's possible in journey personalization, while changing consumer expectations are reshaping how brands need to interact with their audiences.

The future of customer journeys is being dramatically reshaped by technologies that can predict and respond to customer needs in real-time. Imagine a journey that automatically adapts based on subtle signals in customer behavior and offers not just based on past actions, but on predicted future needs. This isn't science fiction; it's already happening in pioneering companies that use AI to craft uniquely personalized experiences for each customer.

Yet amidst this technological revolution, we're witnessing a counterintuitive trend: the rising importance of human connection.

As **automation** becomes more prevalent, customers increasingly value authentic, human-centered interactions. The most successful brands of tomorrow will be those that master this balance: using technology to enable more meaningful human connections rather than replace them.

Privacy considerations are also reshaping how we think about customer journeys. With growing awareness and regulation around data usage, brands must become more transparent and intentional about how they collect and use customer information. The future belongs to companies that can create compelling, personalized experiences while respecting and protecting customer privacy.

Future customer journeys won't be defined by platform or device but will flow naturally across touchpoints, following customers through their daily lives. Voice interfaces, augmented reality, and ambient computing will create new types of interactions that feel less like traditional marketing and more like helpful companions on the customer's path.

Perhaps most significantly, we're seeing a shift toward what might be called "journey co-creation," where customers have more control over how they interact with brands.

Rather than following predetermined paths, customers will increasingly expect to shape their own journeys, choosing how and when they engage with brands. This requires a fundamental rethinking of how we design customer experiences, moving from linear journeys to more flexible, customer-directed experiences.

The rise of community-driven commerce is another force shaping future customer journeys. Brands are becoming platforms for connection, where the value comes not just from the product or service but from the community of users around it. This transforms the traditional customer journey into something more collaborative and social, where peer interactions become as important as brand communications.

As we look ahead, one thing becomes clear: the future of customer journeys will be defined not by the technologies we use, but by how we use them to serve genuine human needs and desires. Success will come to brands that can harness these new capabilities while staying true to the timeless principles of human connection, trust, and value creation.

In today's complex digital landscape, the brands that thrive aren't necessarily those with the biggest budgets or the most advanced technology. Instead, *they're the ones that understand how to weave together meaningful experiences that resonate with their customers' lives.* They recognize that every email, every social media interaction, and every customer service call is an opportunity to strengthen the relationship between brand and customer.

In the end, the most successful customer journeys aren't those that simply lead to a purchase. They're the ones that leave customers feeling understood, valued, and eager to continue their relationship with your brand. As we move forward into an increasingly complex and connected world, this human-centered approach to customer journeys will become not just an advantage, but a necessity.

PSYCHOLOGICAL TRIGGERS

Authors have always found compelling ways to engage readers through plot, character, and world building, but by consciously incorporating psychological triggers into storytelling, we can create even deeper resonance that makes stories truly unforgettable. You've likely encountered books that stayed with you long after reading, touching something fundamental in your experience of being human.

The challenge lies not just in crafting good sentences or plotting engaging storylines, but in weaving psychological elements that tap into readers' natural emotional responses. Rather than trying to force engagement through dramatic events or beautiful prose alone, psychological triggers work with readers' innate processing of storylines, making emotional connection feel natural and inevitable.

Consider how you become invested in a story. You don't continue reading just because the writing is polished, or the plot is clever. Instead, you go through a journey of discovery, forming emotional connections with characters and situations that mirror deep human experiences. This same principle applies to crafting scenes and character arcs that truly resonate.

The key difference between technically proficient writing and deeply affecting storytelling lies in the depth of psychological engagement. While basic craft focuses on clear narrative and compelling events, psychological triggers build emotional investment. They create a foundation of authentic human experience that makes readers not just intellectually engaged but viscerally connected to your story.

This approach requires understanding five crucial types of psychological triggers that influence how readers process storylines. Each trigger serves a specific purpose in building authentic narrative resonance, and when used together, they create a comprehensive framework for writing stories that stay with readers long after the last page.

BUILDING MEANINGFUL CONNECTIONS

At their heart, successful stories create deep connections through layers of meaning and emotional resonance. Just as a garden grows through careful cultivation rather than mechanical planting, stories flourish when each element is thoughtfully developed to engage readers on multiple levels. Your scenes and characters should invite readers to explore, discover, and connect with the deeper truths woven throughout your narrative.

When you move beyond surface-level storytelling to create psychological depth, readers transform from passive observers into engaged participants in the journey you've crafted. They become invested not just in plot outcomes, but in the thematic and emotional discoveries along the way. This is the difference between writing a story and creating an experience that stays with readers.

Consider how the most memorable stories work. They don't just present events, they create spaces for readers to explore meaning, discover connections, and engage with ideas that resonate with their own experiences. Each scene serves multiple purposes, operating on both plot and psychological levels simultaneously.

The magic happens when you view your story elements as opportunities for deeper engagement rather than just plot devices. Character choices, setting details, and even dialogue can tap into fundamental human experiences and emotions. When readers connect on this level, they naturally invest in the journey you're creating.

This approach requires understanding that every story element is an opportunity to deepen psychological engagement. Whether through character relationships, thematic exploration, or emotional revelations, each component should contribute to the reader's deeper experience of the story.

Think about the stories that have stayed with you longest. Is it just their plots you remember, or the way they made you feel part of something larger? This same principle applies to your writing. When you focus on creating meaningful psychological resonance, reader engagement naturally follows.

The key is authenticity in how you develop these psychological elements. Readers can sense when emotional moments feel forced versus organically developed. This authenticity, combined with deliberate use of psychological triggers, creates stories that feel both natural and profound.

We're about to explore specific psychological triggers that make this approach work but remember: the foundation of all memorable stories lies in genuine psychological resonance. Without this foundation, even the cleverest plots or beautiful prose will fail to truly move readers.

WHY DO WE NEED PSYCHOLOGICAL TRIGGERS?

Traditional writing often focuses on what we might call "surface engagement," which are those story elements that immediately grab readers through clear genre markers, familiar tropes, or compelling hooks. While these elements are important, they only reach readers already primed to connect with your type of story.

Focusing solely on these surface elements means missing opportunities to create deeper resonance. Even if someone enjoys fantasy novels, they might not fully engage with your fantasy story without deeper psychological anchoring. The key lies in weaving multiple layers of psychological connection throughout your narrative.

This is where psychological triggers become crucial. Instead of relying on plot or genre conventions alone, we use five powerful elements to create multiple pathways for reader engagement:

- Core Wounds
- Pleasure and Pain Inducers
- X-Factors
- Connection Deepeners
- Button-Pushers

Each trigger addresses different aspects of how readers connect with the story, allowing your narrative to resonate on multiple psychological levels simultaneously.

The more psychological layers you build into your story, the more opportunities you create for meaningful connection. One reader might connect with your character's internal struggles (Core Wounds), while another responds to the thematic exploration of fundamental fears. Someone else might be drawn in by the unique perspective you bring (X-Factor), while others engage with the transformational journey you've crafted.

By moving beyond surface engagement, you're not just writing a story, you're creating an experience that resonates on multiple psychological levels. This approach requires more careful crafting, but it results in something far more valuable: stories that stay with readers long after they finish the last page.

These psychological elements work together to create stories that don't just entertain but leave lasting impressions that change how readers see themselves and their world.

UNDERSTANDING CORE WOUNDS

When we talk about core wounds in writing, we're exploring something far deeper than simple pain points or customer needs. These are the fundamental emotional injuries that shape how people view themselves and interact with the world. Think of them as the deep grooves in our psychological landscape, carved by experiences often dating back to childhood.

Core wounds manifest in six primary transformational paths, each representing a journey from pain to healing:

- **Rejection to Acceptance:** This wound centers on the deep human need to belong. People carrying this wound constantly seek validation, afraid they'll never truly fit in. Your writing might speak to how your work helps readers find their tribe or validates their experiences.

- **Control to Surrender:** Here we find people struggling with uncertainty and chaos. They grip tightly to whatever they can control, often missing the beauty of letting go. Your content could explore how embracing uncertainty leads to unexpected gifts.
- **Abandonment to Integration:** This wound touches on our fear of being left behind or forgotten. Those carrying this wound often struggle to trust or form deep connections. Your messaging might focus on building lasting relationships and creating stable foundations.
- **Shame to Honor:** Perhaps one of the most profound wounds, shame makes people feel inherently flawed or unworthy. Your writing could demonstrate pathways to self-acceptance and pride in one's authentic self.
- **Betrayal to Devotion:** This wound impacts how people trust and form relationships. Those carrying it often expect to be let down or deceived. Your content might explore themes of loyalty, trust-building, and genuine connection.
- **Injustice to Equality:** This wound stems from experiences of unfairness or discrimination. People carrying it are highly attuned to power imbalances and seek level playing fields.

The power of understanding these core wounds lies in how we use them. It's not about exploiting pain points, creating genuine paths to healing. When you structure your story around addressing these wounds, you're not just writing a book; you're offering a transformation both to your character and your reader.

If you're writing a fantasy novel about an outcast who finds their place in the world, you're speaking directly to the rejection-to-acceptance wound. The key is authenticity. *Readers can sense when you're genuinely addressing their deep emotional needs versus simply using their pain to make a sale.* This is why the most effective books often come from authors who have worked through these same wounds themselves. They can speak to both the pain and the possibility of healing from a place of genuine understanding.

What makes core wounds such a powerful foundation for writing is their universality. While we might experience them differently, these fundamental hurts are part of the human experience. By acknowledging and addressing them respectfully, we create books that resonate on a profound level, making readers feel truly seen and understood.

The goal isn't to fix these wounds. That's beyond the scope of what we do as writers. Instead, we're creating safe spaces where these wounds can be acknowledged, understood, and gently tended. This approach transforms writing into a healing journey that benefits both author and reader.

PLEASURE AND PAIN INDUCERS

At our core, humans experience the world through two fundamental lenses: pleasure and pain. These emotional experiences drive our decision-making in profound and often unconscious ways. Understanding how to work with these emotional drivers can transform your writing from mere promotion to meaningful engagement.

We might consider ourselves "logical creatures," but emotions drive decisions, and logic justifies them after the fact. You can come up with rational reasons to justify any decision, but the initial impulse was purely emotional. This is how the human brain works. *Emotion leads and logic follows.*

In writing, pleasure and pain inducers serve as emotional resonance points. They help readers connect with your work on a visceral level. A romance novel doesn't just tell a love story. It taps into the pleasure of falling in love and the pain of loneliness. A thriller doesn't just offer suspense. It plays with the pleasure of solving mysteries and the pain of uncertainty.

The key is understanding that these emotional triggers aren't meant to manipulate. Instead, they're meant to create authentic connections. *When you share your own experiences with pleasure and pain in your writing, you're inviting readers into a shared emotional space.* You're saying, "I understand what you're feeling because I've felt it too."

Consider how this works in practice. Let's say you're writing a self-help book about personal growth. Instead of just focusing on its features ("10 chapters of actionable advice!"), you might tap into:

The pain points:

- The frustration of feeling stuck
- The exhaustion of trying and failing
- The fear of never reaching your potential

And balance them with pleasure points:

- The joy of breakthrough moments
- The satisfaction of personal progress
- The excitement of discovering new possibilities

It's a balance, and they work best in parity with each other. You can't focus too heavily on pain points by creating writing that feels heavy and depressing, nor can you lean too far into pleasure, making promises that feel unrealistic. The magic lies in acknowledging the pain while illuminating the path to pleasure.

Your writing should create an emotional arc. Start by showing readers you understand their current emotional state (*often pain-based*). Then, guide them through the possibility of transformation, painting a vivid picture of what could be (*pleasure-based*). Finally, position your work as the bridge between these two states.

This approach works because it mirrors how we naturally process emotional experiences. Most of the time, we don't jump directly from pain to pleasure. We need to feel understood in our current state before we're ready to envision change. Your writing should honor this journey, creating space for both the current reality and the potential future.

One powerful technique is to develop emotional echoes. These are recurring themes or phrases that resonate with both the pain and pleasure aspects of your readers' experiences. For example, "From overwhelmed to overjoyed," or, "Transform your struggle into strength." These paired concepts create emotional bookends that readers can relate to.

It's important to note here that readers in some genres (*like romcom*) want very little pain and a lot of pleasure while readers of others (*like grimdark*) are there, at least partially, for the pain.

Remember, *every reader is on their own emotional journey.* Your job isn't to force them into feeling certain emotions, but to create writing that recognizes and respects where they are while gently illuminating where they could be. This approach builds trust and creates deeper connections than traditional feature-focused writing ever could.

By unlocking more pain and pleasure inducers in your writing, you can give permission for more people to read your work. Maybe one pain inducer is clear from your cover and blurb, but if you embed several more into your work, and unearth them through your writing, you can exponentially increase your market.

X-FACTOR

In today's market, being good at writing is not enough anymore. The market is flooded with talented authors, all vying for readers' attention. This is where the X-Factor comes into play. It positions you several steps ahead of your audience and establishes you as someone worth following, not just another voice in the crowd.

Think of the X-Factor as your unique value proposition, but with a crucial twist. *It's not just about what makes you different, but what makes you a natural leader for your specific audience.* When you properly establish your X-Factor, readers don't just buy your books. They join your movement.

Consider Brandon Sanderson. He's not just writing fantasy novels, but an entire universe of intricate magic all while hosting a community filled with hundreds of thousands of loyal readers. His X-Factor isn't just his writing ability but lies in his ability to make readers feel like they're part of the creative journey.

The X-Factor works by providing two critical elements: heroes to look up to and "aha moments" that transform readers' lives. These aha moments are particularly powerful because they create lasting connections.

When a reader experiences an insight or breakthrough because of your work, they're much more likely to become a loyal follower.

Your X-Factor isn't just about your credentials or achievements. It's about how you use your experience and expertise to inspire action in others. *If you've overcome significant obstacles to write your books, that journey becomes part of your X-Factor.* If you have unique professional experience that informs your writing, that's part of your X-Factor too.

The most effective way to establish your X-Factor is through what I call "leadership positioning." *This means consistently demonstrating not just what you know, but how that knowledge or experience benefits your readers.* It's about creating a clear path between your expertise and your readers' desired outcomes.

One of the hardest truths for authors to process is that none of this, not one word that you've ever written, no matter how personal, is about you. It's all about your reader using your work as a conduit to explore their own transformation.

Your X-Factor should make it clear why you're the right person to guide readers through this transformation. This might mean sharing behind-the-scenes glimpses of your creative process, explaining how your life experiences inform your writing, or demonstrating your deep understanding of the genres or topics you write about.

Importantly, your X-Factor should inspire readers to listen and take action. If you're writing historical fiction, your X-Factor might be your unique approach to research that brings forgotten stories to life. If you're writing self-help, it might be your proven method for achieving specific results. Whatever it is, it should give readers a compelling reason to choose your work over others in your field.

The beauty of developing a strong X-Factor is that it makes marketing feel more natural. Instead of awkwardly promoting your books, you're sharing valuable insights and experiences that naturally lead readers to want more of what you offer. It transforms marketing from pushing sales to pulling readers into your world.

CONNECTION DEEPENERS

Think of Connection Deepeners as bridges between you and your readers, just not the mass-produced steel and concrete kind. These are more like handcrafted wooden bridges, each one unique, built with care and attention to the specific landscape they span.

The fascinating thing about Connection Deepeners is that they work by creating resonance with your audience in ways that go beyond just your books. When used effectively, they help readers feel truly seen and understood, often in ways they didn't realize they needed.

Meeting readers where they are is crucial to this process. This means understanding that every reader comes to your work with their own context, their own struggles, their own hopes. Instead of expecting readers to adapt to your world, you're creating points of connection that feel natural and intuitive to them.

What makes Connection Deepeners particularly powerful is that they give readers a shared language to communicate with each other. *When you create terms, phrases, or concepts that resonate with your audience, you're not just building individual connections, you're fostering a community.* Consider how Terry Pratchett fans immediately understand references to "The Luggage" or how Stephen King readers share a special understanding of *The Dark Tower*. These aren't just story elements, but community touchstones.

What's often overlooked is how Connection Deepeners work beyond the obvious fan-author relationship. *They create reader-to-reader bonds that strengthen your entire community.* This is why successful authors often find their readers forming book clubs, fan groups, or online communities without direct author involvement. The connections you create become self-sustaining.

The most powerful aspect of Connection Deepeners is their ability to make readers feel like their truest selves in your community. This isn't about creating a false sense of belonging, it's about providing safe spaces where readers can explore, express, and embrace who they really are. When readers feel this level of acceptance and understanding, they become more than just consumers of your work, they become active participants in your author journey.

Remember that scene in *Dead Poets Society* where students stand on their desks to see the world differently?

That's what Connection Deepeners do. They offer new perspectives, new ways of seeing and understanding, that readers carry with them long after they've finished your books.

BUTTON-PUSHERS

Button-Pushers are those subtle yet powerful elements that transform interest into action. They're what makes someone stop scrolling, click through, and ultimately make a purchase. But they're not just about driving sales; they're about creating those magical moments where a reader thinks, "Yes, this is exactly what I've been looking for."

I call this process of realization the "snap, snap, snap." Picture what happens at a successful book signing. There's that moment when someone sees your book and something catches their eye. That's the first "snap," or *the stop.* Then, they read the back cover or a random passage that speaks directly to them. That's the second "snap," or *the click.* Finally, they walk to the register, book in hand. That's the third "snap," or *the buy.* These three snaps aren't random. They're carefully orchestrated moments of connection.

What makes Button-Pushers so powerful is their ability to work at a subconscious level. When you use them effectively, readers don't feel pushed or manipulated. They feel drawn in, compelled by their own curiosity and desire. It's like creating a path of breadcrumbs that leads readers naturally to the next step.

Button-Pushers aren't about being clever or manipulative. They're about being so genuinely compelling that readers can't help but want to engage further. When you share a story that resonates deeply with your audience, when you tap into their genuine desires and aspirations, you're not pushing buttons - you're opening doors.

The real magic happens when Button-Pushers align with genuine value. Your goal isn't just to get someone to buy your book; it's to ensure they're genuinely excited to read it. Think about how Netflix gets you to watch "just one more episode" - not through force, but by understanding and delivering exactly what you want next.

Used effectively, Button-Pushers help potential readers self-identify. They think, "This author gets me," or, "This is exactly what I need right now." When this happens, you've created something powerful, a connection that goes beyond the transaction to create genuine anticipation and excitement.

Remember, the ultimate goal isn't just to make the sale, it's to create such a compelling case for your work that readers can't wait to dive in.

UNDERSTANDING LIFE'S TRANSITIONS

Above psychological triggers, one other powerful thing to consider with your writing is focusing on specific *transition points.* Every significant change in life creates a moment of psychological openness, a time when people are more receptive to new ideas, solutions, and perspectives.

Think of transitions like a house during renovation. When the walls are stripped bare and the floors are being replaced, that's when you can make the biggest changes. Similarly, when people are going through major life transitions, their normal patterns and resistances are disrupted, creating unique opportunities for meaningful connection.

What makes transitions such powerful moments to focus? During times of change, people experience what psychologists call "identity plasticity" when their sense of self becomes more flexible and open to transformation. This isn't just about being more likely to buy. It's about being more receptive to deep, meaningful engagement with content that speaks to their current experience.

Consider the common transitions we all face: graduating from school, starting a new job, entering or leaving relationships, becoming parents, changing careers, moving cities, facing health challenges, or retiring. Each of these moments creates a psychological state where people actively seek guidance, understanding, and support. They're not just looking for solutions; they're looking for meaning and connection during times of uncertainty.

The key to leveraging transition points effectively lies in understanding their emotional architecture. Every transition contains three essential elements:

First, there's *the letting go phase,* where people release old patterns, identities, or situations. This often involves grief, uncertainty, and anxiety, even when the change is positive. Your writing can acknowledge and validate these complex emotions.

Second comes the *neutral zone*, the uncomfortable period between the old and the new. This is where people feel most vulnerable but also most open to new perspectives. Your content can provide guidance and reassurance during this crucial phase.

Finally, there's *the new beginning* where people establish fresh patterns and identities. This is when they're actively seeking tools, communities, and frameworks to support their emerging reality.

What makes transitions particularly powerful is that people in transition are actively engaged in self-directed change. *They're not passive consumers waiting to be sold to, but active seekers looking for resources that speak to their experience.* This creates natural openings for authentic connection and meaningful engagement.

Your task as a marketer is to identify which transition points align naturally with your work. What moments of change does your content speak to? When are people most likely to need what you offer? Understanding these intersections allows you to create books that feel less like telling a story and more like extending a helping hand at exactly the right moment.

EXAMPLES THAT TIE IT ALL TOGETHER

Now that we have all the pieces, let's talk about transitions and their psychological triggers in a way that feels more concrete.

THE NEW PARENT

Think about someone who's just become a new parent. They're in a massive life transition, probably sleep-deprived, overwhelmed, and questioning everything. This is a perfect moment to connect with readers because during transitions, people actively seek solutions and support. They're hungry for guidance.

Their core wound might be feeling utterly unprepared or isolated. So, if you write parenting books, you don't just market your "how-to" guide. You speak to that deep feeling of uncertainty. You might share your own stumbling first weeks of parenthood (*Connection Deepener*), demonstrate your expertise through specific, relatable situations (*X-Factor*), and show the pleasure of moving from chaos to confidence.

Or consider someone going through a divorce. They're dealing with a profound sense of failure (*Core Wound*), questioning their identity, and facing an uncertain future. If you write self-discovery novels or personal growth books, this transition moment is rich with potential connection points. Your books might emphasize the journey from betrayal to trust, from brokenness to wholeness.

Career changes are another powerful transition point. Someone leaving corporate life to start their own business is experiencing multiple psychological triggers simultaneously, like fear of failure, dreams of independence, and a need for validation. If you write business books or even fiction about personal reinvention, this transition provides natural connection points.

The key is recognizing that transitions create openings for deeper engagement because people in transition are actively looking for:

- Validation of their feelings
- Guidance through uncertainty
- Hope for the future
- Community of others in similar situations

CAREER BURNOUT

Let's explore another powerful transition moment: career burnout. This is fascinating because it combines both professional and deeply personal psychological triggers.

Picture someone in their mid-thirties who's achieved everything they thought they wanted. They have a good job, decent salary, and respectable title. But they're exhausted, unfulfilled, and quietly wondering "Is this all there is?" This transition point is particularly rich because it involves multiple core wounds: the shame of feeling ungrateful for a "good" job, the fear of starting over, and often a deep sense of betrayal (*either by the system or their own choices*).

If you write inspirational fiction or career transformation books, this transition creates natural connection points. The core wound here isn't just about career frustration, it's about identity. Who are you when the career you've built stops defining you? This is where pleasure and pain inducers become incredibly powerful.

The pain points are vivid: Sunday night anxiety, feeling trapped in golden handcuffs, watching life pass by in endless Zoom meetings. But the pleasure points are equally compelling: rediscovering passion, feeling alive again, building something meaningful. Your writing might weave these together, showing understanding of both the current pain and the potential for transformation.

Your X-Factor might come from having made this journey yourself, or from guiding others through it. You're not just offering escape; you're providing a roadmap through the wilderness of career reinvention. This resonates particularly strongly because people in career transitions are often looking for both practical guidance and emotional support.

The Connection Deepeners here could focus on shared experiences that often go unspoken: the guilt of wanting more, the fear of disappointing family, the secret relief of finally admitting you need change. When you name these experiences, readers feel seen and understood, often for the first time.

Button-Pushers in this context might focus on the cost of staying stuck versus the potential of change. Not in a manipulative way, but by reflecting real questions your readers are already asking themselves, "What's the real price of another year in this job?" "What possibilities am I never giving myself permission to explore?"

This transition point is especially powerful because it often coincides with other life transitions: relationships, health, personal identity. It's a moment when people are particularly receptive to new ideas and perspectives, making them more likely to engage deeply with content that speaks to their experience.

During career burnout transitions, people are actively seeking:

- Validation that their dissatisfaction is legitimate and significant, not just ingratitude or weakness
- Evidence that change is possible, not just inspirational stories, but concrete paths forward
- Permission to prioritize fulfillment over traditional metrics of success
- Frameworks to help them imagine and build a different future

MOVING TO A NEW CITY

Let's explore the transition of moving to a new city, a moment that combines external change with profound internal shifts.

Picture someone who's just accepted a job in a new city. On the surface, it's about logistics, like finding an apartment, learning new routes, and setting up utilities. But underneath, this person is wrestling with deeper questions about identity, community, and belonging. They're literally and figuratively mapping out a new life.

This transition is particularly rich because it often involves mourning what's left behind while simultaneously building something new. The core wound here centers on belonging, the fear of being perpetually "new," of losing established connections, of having to rebuild from scratch in an unfamiliar environment.

If you write contemporary fiction, self-help, or even city-specific guides, this transition creates powerful connection opportunities. You're catching readers at a moment when their normal support systems are disrupted and they're actively seeking new connections and guidance. The pleasure and pain points here are deeply intertwined: the excitement of new possibilities exists alongside the anxiety of unknown challenges.

Your X-Factor might be having made multiple successful moves yourself, understanding the emotional landscape of relocation, or having deep knowledge of building community in new places. You're not just offering practical advice; you're providing emotional scaffolding for this major life change.

During relocation transitions, people are actively seeking:

- Reassurance that their mix of excitement and grief is normal and valid
- Practical tools for building social connections from scratch
- Guidance on maintaining old relationships while creating new ones
- Ways to preserve their identity while adapting to a new environment

TRANSFORMING YOUR BOOK INTO A GRIPPING READ

As we've explored the intricate landscape of psychological triggers, one fundamental truth emerges: successful books are not about selling but about connecting. It's about creating a bridge between your work and the readers who need it most, understanding that every book is more than just a product. It's a potential transformation waiting to happen.

The strategies we've discussed—*Core Wounds, Pleasure and Pain Inducers, X-Factor, Connection Deepeners*, and *Button-Pushers*—are not manipulative tactics, but genuine pathways to meaningful engagement. They represent a profound shift from traditional approaches that treat readers as passive consumers to a more holistic model that sees readers as active participants in a shared journey.

Remember, your book is a vehicle for connection, not just information or entertainment. Every reader comes to your work with their own story, their own struggles, and their own hopes. Your books should honor that complexity, creating spaces where readers feel truly seen and understood.

The most powerful writing happens when you are trying to serve. This means:

- Deeply understanding the transitions and challenges your readers face
- Sharing your authentic journey with vulnerability and courage
- Creating content that goes beyond your books to address fundamental human experiences
- Building communities that support and uplift readers

Ultimately, successful writing is about trust. Trust that develops not through aggressive promotion, but through consistent, genuine connection. It's about showing readers that you understand them, that you're committed to their growth and transformation, and that your work is a tool for their own personal journey.

Your words have power, not just on the page, but in the lives of those who read them. Writing, when done with empathy and insight, becomes an extension of that power. It's an invitation, a bridge, a helping hand extended to readers who are seeking something more than just another book.

So, step forward with confidence. Your writing is not about shouting into the void but about creating meaningful dialogue. It's about turning the solitary act of writing into a collaborative experience of human connection. In a world hungry for authenticity, your genuine approach will not just sell books. It will create a lasting impact.

BUILDING AN AUDIENCE FROM SCRATCH

I have a sizable audience now, but it wasn't always that way. For years, I launched books to crickets again and again. My first two crowdfunding launches on Indiegogo didn't even make 20% of their goal…combined!

Over time, I found strategies to help me turn it around, and they turned me from launching a book or project to crickets into an author with a dedicated fanbase that gobbled up my work, helping me raise over $600,000 on Kickstarter and over a million dollars on creative projects throughout my career.

Over time, my revenue has grown from a few thousand a year to hundreds of thousands every year, and the strategies I use now aren't much different from the ones that helped me turn my whole career around.

The secret? Learning how to build your audience. If you have a fanbase ready to buy from you, you have an author business. It's that simple. This guide will walk you through the steps to build an audience from scratch, one that's primed to buy your books. Finding your superfans.

This isn't about vague advice or quick fixes. It's about practical, actionable steps that create leverage and turn casual readers into devoted fans.

FIND YOUR BRAND

I've probably already lost you, haven't I? There's nothing writers like talking about less than their brand, which is wild because the next entry on that list is anything else related to marketing.

Do you know what the easiest way to not have to do marketing is? To develop a strong brand that speaks for you when you can't speak for yourself. ***The louder your brand screams to the right reader, the more you'll be able to sit back and let organic reach do a lot of the work for you.***

Everyone has a brand, whether they realize it or not. Your brand is the sum total of associations people have with you and your work. It's not just about a logo or a color scheme. It's about the emotions, ideas, and values that come to mind when someone thinks of you.

Even your grandmother has a brand. It's true. Close your eyes and think of your grandmother. What feelings come to mind? What imagery? What colors? All of that is your grandmother's brand. We're just taking those feelings and making it explicit.

Let's consider the stark contrast between Abercrombie & Fitch and Hot Topic. Both are clothing retailers, but they appeal to vastly different audiences.

Abercrombie & Fitch cultivates an image of preppy, clean-cut Americana. Their ideal customer likely values fitting in, following trends, and projecting a polished image.

On the other hand, Hot Topic embraces counterculture, alternative fashion, and pop culture fandom. Their ideal customer probably prides themselves on standing out, expressing individuality, and rejecting mainstream norms.

These brands aren't just selling clothes, they're selling identities. In high school, there were Abercrombie kids and Hot Topic kids. You could tell them from a mile away, and rarely did the two intersect.

Identifying your brand, and the identity of your ideal reader, is exactly what you're doing as an author. Your books aren't just stories; they're experiences that help your readers understand themselves and their place in the world.

The more clearly you can define your brand and align it with your ideal readers, the easier it becomes to attract the right audience. This alignment creates a powerful resonance. When readers encounter your work, they should feel a sense of recognition, not just of your stories, but of themselves.

The expression of that identity is your brand. It's not even really about you. It's about the identity of the person reading your work and how to attract them.

Think about the emotions and ideas you want to associate with your brand. Are you the voice of the outsider, the rebel, the dreamer? Or perhaps you're the guide for the curious, the explorer of hidden truths? Whatever it is, make it clear and consistent across all your work and communications.

So, how do we find our brand?

1. INTERVIEW PEOPLE WHO FIT YOUR TARGET DEMOGRAPHIC

Even if you don't have readers, you've likely been on social media for a long time and know the people who seem to resonate with your work. Start there, *especially* if they are readers. They don't have to be readers, though, because they are still reading your posts and engaging with your content.

I would stay away from people you know well or have a vested interest in lying to you; not that they *want* to lie to you, but they *do* want to protect you, *even if it means lying*.

This is about having real conversations with the types of readers you want to attract. It's not just a quick survey, but an in-depth exploration of their world. When you talk to these potential readers, pay attention to:

- The specific words and phrases they use to describe their interests. Do they call themselves "bookworms" or "lit nerds"? Are they "pop culture junkies" or "fandom enthusiasts"?
- The challenges they face in their daily lives. What frustrates them? What keeps them up at night?
- Their aspirations and dreams. What do they hope to achieve or experience?
- The other media they consume. What shows do they watch? What music do they listen to?
- Their purchasing habits. How do they decide which books to buy? What factors influence their decisions?

These interviews can be formal or informal. You might set up structured interviews or simply engage in conversations at conventions, book clubs, or online forums. The key is to listen more than you speak and to dig deeper than surface-level answers.

2. OBSERVE THEIR BEHAVIOR ONLINE

In today's digital age, your ideal readers are likely leaving a trail of breadcrumbs online. By observing their behavior, you can gain insights into their preferences and habits. Once you identify who in your existing network already resonates with your work, here's what to look for:

- Which social media platforms do they use most frequently? Are they more active on Instagram, Twitter, TikTok, or somewhere else?
- What types of content do they engage with? Do they share memes, participate in writing prompts, or discuss fan theories?
- Who are their influencers? Which authors, celebrities, or thought leaders do they follow and interact with?
- What hashtags do they use? This can give you insight into how they categorize their interests.
- How do they talk about books they love (or hate)? Pay attention to the criteria they use to judge a book.
- What online communities are they part of? Look at forums, Facebook groups, or subreddits related to your genre.

This observation should be ongoing. Online trends and behaviors can shift quickly, so stay tuned in to your audience's digital habits.

3. TEST DIFFERENT MESSAGING AND BRANDING

This is where you start to apply what you've learned. It's an iterative process of trying out different approaches and seeing what sticks. Here's how to go about it:

- Create different versions of your author bio, each emphasizing different aspects of your brand. Which one gets the most positive response?
- Experiment with various taglines or elevator pitches for your books. Which ones make people's eyes light up with interest?
- Try out different visual styles for your book covers or author photos. Which ones seem to attract the most attention from your target audience?
- Post different types of content on your social media or blog. Do your potential readers engage more with behind-the-scenes writing snippets, character discussions, or broader topics related to your genre?
- If you have an email list, try A/B testing your subject lines and content. What gets people to open and click through?

The key here is to track your results meticulously. ***Don't just go with your gut feeling***. Look at the hard data of likes, shares, comments, and, most importantly, conversions to sales or mailing list sign-ups.

This process isn't about changing who you are as an author. It's about finding the most effective way to communicate your authentic self to the readers who will appreciate you most. It's a journey of discovery - both of your audience and of how to best present your unique author brand to the world.

Thoroughly exploring these three areas, you'll gain a deep, nuanced understanding of your ideal customer. This knowledge will inform every aspect of your author business, from the stories you write to how you market them. It's the foundation upon which you'll build your loyal, engaged audience.

Remember, *a strong brand doesn't try to appeal to everyone.* It's okay, even necessary, to repel some people in order to strongly attract others. Your goal is to be the Abercrombie to your preppy crowd, or the Hot Topic to your alternative scene.

This is how you'll find the readers who *resonate most with your work* and are *most likely to voraciously read everything you write*. Yes, some people will cross over and read multiple types of books, but they'll still need to be in the right mindset for your book. Therefore, it's best to define yourself really well so they can find you when their mood shifts.

By understanding and refining your brand, you're essentially creating a beacon for your ideal readers. You're making it easier for them to find you amidst the noise of the publishing world. And when they do find you, they'll recognize you as 'their' author, the one who truly gets them.

4. PLANT WHERE YOU ARE MOST COMFORTABLE

The truth about "audience building" is that you can build an audience anywhere and in any format. What matters most is choosing a platform that aligns with your strengths and where your ideal readers are likely to be.

Think of it like choosing the right soil for a plant. Some plants thrive in sandy soil, others in clay. Similarly, some authors flourish on Facebook, while others find their groove on YouTube or blogging platforms. The key is to find your optimal environment.

When selecting your platform, consider these factors:

1. **Your natural communication style:** Are you better at writing short, snappy messages? Long-form content? Visual storytelling? Choose a platform that plays to your strengths.
2. **The preferences of your ideal audience:** Remember those readers we identified in Step 1? Where do they hang out online? That's where you need to be.
3. **The platform's algorithm:** Each social media platform has its own algorithm that determines what content gets shown to users. Understanding how these algorithms work can help you create content that's more likely to reach your audience.
4. **Your goals:** What are you trying to achieve? Building an email list? Driving book sales? Different platforms are better suited for different goals.

Once you've chosen your platform, commit to it fully. Pick one platform and go hard on it for three months. If it works, keep at it until you get organic traction.

Your real goal isn't just to build an audience on a third-party platform. *It's to get them into your own ecosystem.* Think of social media platforms as fishing ponds. You're there to catch fish (readers), but you want to bring them back to your own pond (your website/mailing list) where you have full control.

I've been running an email list since 2015, after my first big project delivered to backers, and, in that time, I've only missed 1-2 weekly emails to my audience. I'm not great at social media marketing, but I'm incredible at finding the right people, sorting them from the rest, and then holding onto them for dear life. A lot of my readers have been following me for most, or all, of those years. It's literally saved my life, and my career, a dozen times.

This is where the concept of leverage comes into play. *The bigger your audience, the more you can do with less work*. People with chronic illnesses ask how to become successful with their limited energy and it *always* comes back to building leverage.

Everything you do on your chosen platform should be about using that platform's reach and algorithm to bring people to your own space. *It makes no sense to be on a platform unless you're going to use it to create leverage.* If you hate how a platform works, abandon it. The *only* places where you should consider being are places that help you leverage your work.

In practice, this might look like using X to share engaging snippets that lead people to your blog or using Instagram to showcase visual elements of your world that entice people to join your mailing list for more exclusive content.

The key is to always think about how to move people from the platform where you found them to the platforms you own. This is how you build a sustainable author business that isn't at the mercy of algorithm changes or platform policies.

When you've successfully attracted someone to your platform or mailing list, the next challenge is keeping them engaged and nurturing the relationship. Here are some effective strategies for what to say:

1. **Share behind-the-scenes content:** People love feeling like they're getting an exclusive look into your creative process. You might discuss your writing routine, share early drafts or deleted scenes, or explain the inspiration behind certain characters or plot points.

2. **Offer value beyond your books:** Provide content that enriches your readers' lives in some way. This could be writing tips if many of your readers are aspiring authors, book recommendations in your genre, or insights related to the themes of your work.

3. **Create serialized content:** Develop ongoing series of posts or emails that keep readers coming back. This could be a weekly writing prompt, a monthly Q&A session, or a series exploring different aspects of your fictional world.

4. **Share personal stories:** Without oversharing, let your audience get to know you as a person. Share anecdotes about your life, your journey as a writer, or your thoughts on relevant current events. This helps build a more personal connection with your readers.

5. **Curate interesting content:** Become a trusted source of information in your niche. Share articles, videos, or other content that you think your audience would find interesting, always adding your own perspective.

6. **Engage in discussions:** Ask questions, pose thought experiments, or start debates related to your work or genre. Encourage your audience to share their thoughts and engage with each other.

7. **Provide sneak peeks and teasers:** Give your audience glimpses of your upcoming work to build

anticipation. This could be cover reveals, chapter excerpts, or hints about future plot developments.

8. **Celebrate milestones:** Share your successes with your audience, whether it's finishing a draft, hitting a sales goal, or receiving an award. Let them feel part of your journey.
9. **Respond to current events or trends:** If something happening in the world relates to your work or your audience's interests, offer your perspective on it.
10. **Run contests or challenges:** Engage your audience with writing contests, fan art challenges, or other interactive events that get them actively involved with your brand.

Also, pay attention to what resonates with your audience. Track engagement metrics and adjust your content strategy based on what your specific audience responds to most positively. Every audience is unique, so what works for one author might not work for another.

Remember, the key is to balance promotional content with valuable, engaging material that isn't directly selling anything. A good rule of thumb is the 80/20 rule: 80% of your content should provide value, and only 20% should be directly promotional.

By consistently providing value and fostering engagement, you'll keep your audience interested and invested in your work, making them more likely to support you when you do have a new release or product to promote.

5. HELP READERS UNDERSTAND THEMSELVES

People don't just care about your stories for the stories' sake. *They care about how your work helps them understand themselves and their place in the world.* Your writing becomes a lens through which they view their own experiences and emotions.

Think about popular franchises like *Game of Thrones* or *Star Wars*. Fans don't just enjoy the plot. They deeply identify with certain houses or characters. ***They use these stories as a way to express aspects of their own personality.*** The same principle applies to your work, regardless of your genre.

To implement this step effectively:

1. **Create shared language:** Develop terms, phrases, or concepts in your work that readers can adopt to describe their own experiences. This could be character archetypes, made-up words, or unique perspectives on common situations.
2. **Foster community discussions:** Encourage your readers to engage with each other using the context you've provided. This could be through social media, forums, or even in-person events. The goal is for readers to feel part of a community that "gets" them.
3. **Provide frameworks for self-understanding:** Your stories or non-fiction concepts can offer readers new ways to categorize and understand their own traits, experiences, or challenges. This is similar to how personality tests like the Enneagram have become popular - people value tools that help them make sense of themselves.
4. **Connect your work to real-world experiences:** Help readers see how the themes, conflicts, or ideas in your books relate to their daily lives. This makes your work feel more relevant and impactful.
5. **Be vulnerable and authentic:** Share your own journey and how your work has helped you understand

yourself better. This invites readers to do the same and creates a stronger bond between you and your audience.

The goal is not just to entertain or inform, but to give your readers a new context through which they can understand and express themselves. When this clicks into place, your work becomes more than just a book. It becomes part of your readers' identity.

People's favorite books have nothing to do with the words on the page, but with feeling seen and being given language to understand their world better.

This approach creates a deeper, more loyal connection with your audience. ***They're not just buying a book; they're investing in a way of understanding themselves and the world.*** This is how you create superfans who will eagerly await your next release and enthusiastically recommend your work to others.

6. FIND YOUR SUPERFANS

Superfans are the backbone of a successful author business. They're not just casual readers. They're the passionate advocates who will buy everything you produce, spread the word about your work, and form the core of your community.

To understand superfans, we need to think about the sales funnel. Imagine a funnel with a wide top narrowing to a small bottom. At the top, you have a large number of people who might be interested in your work. As we move down the funnel, the number decreases, but the level of engagement increases. At the very bottom are your superfans.

The process of moving people down this funnel is gradual. It starts with *awareness,* which is people simply knowing you exist. Then comes *interest*, where they might follow you on social media or join your mailing list. Next is *engagement*, where they start interacting with your content regularly. After that comes *purchasing*, where they buy your books. But the journey doesn't end there.

The final stage, *where superfans are born*, is when readers become so invested in your work that they feel a personal connection to it. They don't just read your books; they live in the world you've created. They don't just enjoy your writing; they feel that it speaks to them on a deep, personal level.

So how do you find and nurture these superfans? It starts by turning that sales funnel on its side and turning it into a *bowtie funnel.*

BOWTIE FUNNEL

The bow-tie funnel model presents a comprehensive view of the customer journey, from initial awareness to becoming a superfan and brand advocate. Let's break it down step by step:

The left side of the bowtie represents the traditional sales funnel we talked about, with the narrow middle of the bowtie representing the point of sale. *This is where a reader transitions from a prospect to a customer by buying your book.*

The right side of the bowtie is where the superfan journey begins:

1. **Adopt:** The reader starts to incorporate your work into their life, perhaps by talking about it with friends or seeking out more of your content.
2. **Loyalist:** They become a repeat customer, eagerly anticipating and purchasing your new releases.
3. **Advocate:** At this stage, the reader actively promotes your work to others, leaving reviews and recommending your books.
4. **Brand Ambassador:** This is the superfan stage. These readers feel a deep connection to your work and consistently champion your brand.

The circular arrow in the center represents the continuous customer experience. It's a reminder that building superfans is an ongoing process of learning, changing, and improving how you interact with your audience.

To build superfans through this model:

1. **Focus on providing value at every stage.** Even at the 'Attract' stage, you should offer content that enriches your potential readers' lives.
2. **Create smooth transitions between stages.** Make it easy for an 'Engaged' reader to become an 'Adopter' by providing clear next steps and additional content.
3. **Recognize and reward loyalty.** As readers move into the 'Loyalist' and 'Advocate' stages, you can offer exclusive content or experiences to deepen their connection.
4. **Foster community.** Especially in the later stages, create opportunities for your most engaged readers to connect with each other, strengthening their bond with your brand.

5. **Continuously gather feedback and improve.** Use the insights from your superfans to refine your work and your engagement strategies.

Remember, the goal isn't just to move readers through a linear process, but to create a cycle where superfans help attract new readers, starting the process anew. This creates a sustainable ecosystem for your author business.

Practically, we usually create these superfans by building a value ladder.

VALUE LADDER

A *value ladder* is a strategic pricing model that integrates perfectly with the bow-tie funnel concept. Let's explore how these two ideas work together to create a robust author business model. It is essentially a series of offerings at increasing price points and value.

The value ladder for an author might look something like this:

1. Free content like blog posts, short stories on your website, or sample chapters
2. Low-cost ebooks or novellas
3. Full-length print or digital books
4. Signed or special edition books
5. Book bundles or box sets
6. Online writing workshops or courses
7. Exclusive author events or retreats

Now, let's see how this integrates with the bow-tie funnel for an author's audience:

On the left side (traditional funnel):

- **Attract (awareness/interest):** Your free content serves as a gateway. This could be blog posts about your writing process, free short stories set in your book's world, or the first few chapters of your novel available on your website.
- **Nurture (engagement):** Offer low-cost entry points like a $0.99 ebook, novella, or a discounted first-in-series book. This allows readers to sample your writing style with minimal risk.
- **Convert (purchasing):** This is where readers buy your full-length book, whether it's an ebook, paperback, or hardcover.

On the right side (superfan journey):

- **Engage:** After reading your book, fans might seek out signed copies, special editions, or companion books that expand on your world or characters.
- **Adopt:** Engaged readers might invest in a box set of your series or a bundle of your books.
- **Loyalist:** Devoted fans might sign up for your online writing workshop, especially if you write in a genre they aspire to write in themselves.
- **Advocate:** Your superfans might splurge on exclusive author retreats or VIP experiences at book signings.

This model benefits authors in several ways:

1. It provides multiple ways for readers to discover and engage with your work, catering to different levels of interest and commitment.
2. It offers a clear path for readers to deepen their engagement with your writing and your author brand.
3. It allows you to monetize your most devoted fans effectively, creating additional income streams beyond just book sales.

4. It helps build a community around your work, strengthening readers' connection to your brand.
5. It provides ongoing value to your readers between book releases, keeping them engaged and excited about your work.

To implement this as an author:

- Ensure each level of the ladder provides appropriate value. A writing workshop, for instance, should offer unique insights not available in your books or free content.
- Create clear pathways between levels. For example, include information about your online course in the back matter of your books.
- Use insights from higher-level offerings to inform your writing and marketing. Conversations at author retreats might inspire new story ideas or help you understand what readers love most about your work.
- Regularly reassess your offerings. Are there gaps in your value ladder? Could you create a new product or experience to bridge the gap between two existing levels?

By integrating this value ladder into your bow-tie funnel, you're not just moving readers from casual browsers to superfans, you're providing them with ever-increasing value and deepening their relationship with your writing and your author brand. This creates a sustainable author business where your most engaged readers get the most value, and you build a loyal, enthusiastic fan base that supports your writing career long-term.

PUMP VS. FLYWHEEL

Many authors are taught to use social media and other promotional tools like a *pump*, and it's causing them to burn out. The pump-like approach works as follows:

1. You put effort into creating and sharing content on social media (input).
2. In return, you get some engagement, maybe a few book sales (output).
3. This process repeats each time you post or promote.

At first glance, this seems great. You're getting results! ***However, there's a catch: you have to keep pumping constantly.*** The moment you stop putting in effort, the results dry up. It's exhausting and unsustainable in the long run.

A funnel offers an improvement over this pump model. With a funnel, you're creating a system that guides potential readers through a journey:

1. At the top of the funnel, you attract a wide audience with broad appeal content.
2. As they move down the funnel, you provide more specific, valuable content.
3. At the bottom, some of these people become customers, buying your books.

The funnel is better because it's more strategic and efficient than the pump. ***You're not just blindly promoting; you're guiding readers through a thoughtful process.*** However, it still has limitations. It's still somewhat linear, and you need to keep adding new potential readers at the top.

This is where the flywheel comes in, offering an even better model for authors. The flywheel works like this:

1. You put in the initial effort to attract readers and create great work (like with the pump or funnel).
2. But instead of this effort having a one-time effect, it starts a wheel spinning.
3. As readers engage with your work, they become fans.
4. These fans then attract new readers through word-of-mouth, reviews, and sharing.
5. This brings in more readers, who become more fans, spinning the wheel faster.

The key advantage of the flywheel is momentum. Once it's spinning, it takes less effort to keep it going and can even pick up speed on its own. Your past efforts continue to pay off over time, unlike with the pump where you always start from zero.

For authors, this might look like:

- Creating a fantastic book that readers love and recommend (initial push)
- Engaging with your readers through newsletters or social media (keeping it spinning)
- Offering additional value through your website or events (adding more momentum)
- Your excited fans bringing in new readers (the wheel spins faster)

The flywheel model encourages you to focus on creating great experiences for your readers at every touchpoint. This not only sells books but turns readers into advocates who help grow your audience organically.

In essence, while pumps and funnels can produce results, the flywheel offers a more sustainable, momentum-building approach for authors looking to grow their readership and career over the long term.

Why don't people start with a flywheel? *Because it's a lot easier to start with a pump.* When you're trying to find purchase anywhere, a pump gives you something. A flywheel takes an enormous effort to start, but it gets easier over time until it is much easier than a pump further down the road.

It took me years to get started seeing results with a flywheel. Now, I look at my friends who are struggling and see people who used nothing but pumps until they exhausted themselves.

Don't think just because you're not seeing results that you're setting up a flywheel, though. It takes a lot of intention and work to set up a flywheel properly. If you're failing, you might just be doing nothing or pumping a dry well.

Cultivating superfans is about more than just selling books. It's about creating a shared experience, a community, and a sense of belonging. Your superfans should feel like they're part of something special, something that goes beyond just being a consumer of your products.

It's also important to note that you don't need a huge number of superfans to make a significant impact. A small, dedicated group of superfans can be more valuable than a large group of casual readers. They're the ones who will pre-order your books, leave glowing reviews, and enthusiastically recommend your work to others.

By focusing on finding and nurturing your superfans, you're not just building an audience; you're creating a sustainable author business. These are the people who will support you throughout your career, eagerly awaiting each new release and sticking with you through thick and thin.

Remember, the journey from casual reader to superfan is a gradual one. It requires consistent effort, genuine interaction, and a willingness to open up and connect with your audience on a deeper level. But the rewards, both in terms of your career success and the rich, meaningful connections you'll form, are well worth the effort.

Building a successful author business is far more complex and nuanced than simply writing great books. It's about creating a profound connection with readers that transforms them from casual consumers into passionate advocates.

The journey begins with deeply understanding your brand, not as a marketing gimmick, but as a genuine expression of the unique perspective you bring to your work. This means carefully identifying the specific type of reader who will most resonate with your writing, and then deliberately crafting a connection that goes beyond the pages of your books.

By providing readers with a language to understand themselves, by offering increasingly valuable experiences, and by building a community rather than just a customer base, authors can create a sustainable model of engagement that supports their creative work. The most successful authors understand that audience building is not a linear process of constant pushing, but a dynamic, momentum-driven approach more akin to a flywheel. It requires significant initial effort, patience, and a willingness to invest in relationships rather than quick sales.

This means choosing platforms that align with your strengths, creating content that provides genuine value, and focusing on turning readers into superfans who not only buy your books but actively champion your work. It's about creating an ecosystem where your most dedicated readers feel a sense of belonging, where they see your writing as a lens through which they can better understand themselves and their world.

Ultimately, the most powerful marketing is not about selling books, but about creating meaningful connections. Your audience is not just a market to be tapped, but a community to be nurtured.

By approaching your author business with authenticity, strategic thinking, and a genuine desire to provide value, you can build an engaged audience that supports your creative journey for years to come. The path is not easy, and it requires consistent effort, vulnerability, and a deep commitment to your readers.

For those willing to put in the work, the rewards extend far beyond book sales. They include the creation of a lasting, impactful body of work that resonates deeply with those who matter most: your readers.

THE FIVE TIME-TESTED ADOPTION DECISIONS

Whether you're publishing books, building a newsletter audience, or growing your influence, understanding how people decide to buy something is hugely important. Recently, I dove deep into the five essential adoption principles—***Relative Advantage, Compatibility, Simplicity, Observability,*** and ***Trialability***—that help explain why people choose to invest time and attention in your work.

Let's look into each of them more closely.

1. RELATIVE ADVANTAGE: HIGHLIGHT WHAT MAKES YOUR WORK UNIQUE

Your readers have plenty of options, so the key question they ask is: why should they choose your book or newsletter over others? ***Relative Advantage*** is about showing how your work stands out from the rest.

For fiction writers, this might involve demonstrating a fresh take on a familiar genre or showcasing a unique voice. For non-fiction authors, it's about leveraging your specific expertise and offering insights that can't be found elsewhere. Whatever your niche, make it clear what sets your content apart. Whether it's the perspective, the style, or the depth you bring to a subject. This helps readers see the immediate benefit of choosing you.

ACTIONABLE ADVICE

- Identify two or three key aspects of your work that distinguish it from others in your genre. Is it your voice, your expertise, or a fresh angle on a common theme?
- Incorporate these unique elements into your marketing materials, whether that's your book descriptions, social media posts, or newsletter promotions, so that readers immediately understand what makes you different.

2. COMPATIBILITY: MAKE IT EASY TO FIT INTO THEIR LIVES

People tend to buy things that align with their existing preferences, routines, and values. *Compatibility* is the measure of how well your writing fits into the lives of your target audience.

If you're writing in a niche genre, are you marketing to readers who are already invested in that genre? If your audience prefers quick, digestible reads, is your content structured in a way that feels accessible to them? Tailor both your work and your messaging to match the tastes and habits of your intended readers. Compatibility makes it easier for them to engage without hesitation.

ACTIONABLE ADVICE

- Conduct a reader survey or engage in discussions with your current audience to better understand their preferences. What kind of content do they consume? What tone or format resonates with them most?
- Adjust your promotional strategies and content structure to match the feedback. For example, if your audience is busy professionals, highlight the fact that your newsletter is concise and actionable in your marketing.

3. SIMPLICITY: ENSURE AN EFFORTLESS EXPERIENCE

Readers don't want to work too hard to figure out what you're offering. *Simplicity* means making the journey from discovery to reading as seamless as possible.

For your books, this could mean a well-designed, genre-appropriate cover paired with a clear, enticing description. For newsletters, ensure that subscribing is easy and straightforward, without unnecessary steps or confusion. The goal is to remove any friction that could slow down or complicate their engagement. Make it intuitive for them to access your work and understand the value it brings.

ACTIONABLE ADVICE

- Simplify your book descriptions and newsletter landing pages by focusing on one or two key benefits that readers will receive. Avoid overloading them with information.

- Test your subscription or purchasing process yourself. Is it straightforward or are there points where a reader might get confused or give up? Make adjustments to streamline the experience.

4. OBSERVABILITY: SHOW THE BENEFITS OF YOUR WORK

People are more likely to engage when they can see the results others are experiencing. *Observability* is about making those benefits visible.

Encourage readers who love your work to leave reviews on platforms like Amazon, Goodreads, or your website. Positive reviews act as social proof, helping new readers see that your work is valued by others. Sharing testimonials or spotlighting reader feedback on your social media can also create a ripple effect, allowing potential readers to witness the impact of your work before they dive in.

You can also show value by offering sample content, whether it's an excerpt from your latest book or a glimpse of what subscribers will get from your newsletter. By providing a taste of what you have to offer, you give potential readers a way to observe the quality firsthand.

ACTIONABLE ADVICE

- Create a system for requesting and showcasing reader reviews. This could be as simple as sending an email to your mailing list, asking for honest feedback, or encouraging readers to leave a review at the end of your book.

- Share snippets of positive reviews and reader feedback on your social media channels to build social proof and help new readers see the value in your work.

5. TRIALABILITY: LET READERS EXPLORE YOUR WORK FIRST

Trialability refers to giving people a way to experience your work before fully committing to it. Offering a sample or preview of your content can help readers feel more comfortable engaging with something new.

For authors, this could mean sharing the first few chapters of your book or offering a free version of your newsletter. When readers can explore your work without risk, they're more likely to feel confident about their decision to keep going.

ACTIONABLE ADVICE

- Offer a free chapter or preview of your latest book on your website or as part of a newsletter sign-up bonus. This gives potential readers a low-risk way to engage with your work.
- If you offer a paid newsletter, consider creating a "free tier" that provides occasional content, enticing readers to subscribe for full access to all your offerings.

Each of these five adoption decisions work individually to enhance your chances of success, but their real power emerges when they work together. As an author, you should think about how these elements create a seamless experience for your readers from the moment they discover your work to the point where they commit to it.

For example, highlighting your *relative advantage* in a genre that aligns with your audience's preferences (*compatibility*) while making it easy for them to access and understand (*simplicity*) ensures a smooth journey. Then, adding clear value through social proof (*observability*) and low-risk ways to engage (*trialability)* completes the cycle. These strategies don't function in isolation but combine to create a compelling experience that encourages readers to engage with your work on a deeper level.

By synchronizing these five concepts, you'll not only attract more readers but also increase the chances that they become loyal, long-term supporters of your writing.

YOUR WEBSITE IS THE CENTER OF EVERYTHING

If your creative career is a house, your website is the foundation. Not social media. Not Amazon. Not even your email list. Those are all rented rooms in someone else's mansion. But your website? That's yours. And if it sucks, the rest of your business eventually will too.

It doesn't matter how great your books are if your site makes people bounce before they even see a cover. It doesn't matter how many fans you have if they can't find your latest release or sign up for your newsletter. It doesn't matter how brilliant your bonus content is if the delivery page looks like it was built in 2009 by someone's cousin on Wix.

Your website isn't just a brochure. It's the spine of your entire ecosystem. It's where your energy compounds. It's where strangers become subscribers. It's where fans become customers. And it's where customers come back again and again—*if* you build it with intention.

This section is about turning your website into a machine. A smooth, well-oiled, reader-focused system that makes everything else you do more effective. Whether it's your homepage, your store, or your landing pages, you're going to learn how to make every click count.

Let's start at the front door.

YOUR HOMEPAGE IS NOT A RESUME

You're not building a homepage to prove you're a real author. You're building it to turn curious strangers into people who care enough to stick around.

That means your homepage isn't a billboard. It isn't a gallery of your accomplishments. It's not a glorified About page with your awards and a hundred buttons and every single thing you've ever made. It's a tool. A very intentional tool. And it has one job:

Get people to take the next step in your world.

Usually, that next step is joining your email list. Sometimes it's buying your newest book or bundle. But nine times out of ten, your homepage fails if people land there, poke around a bit, and then bounce without doing anything.

So, this chapter is going to teach you how to fix that.

YOU NEED A SIGNUP THAT'S STUPID EASY

Let's star with the most important thing first: if someone visits your homepage and doesn't immediately see a way to get something valuable for free…you've already lost them.

Every homepage needs a very clear, very obvious email signup. Not a generic "Subscribe to my newsletter" in 10-point font buried in the footer. I'm talking about:

- A bold headline like: "Get a free exclusive novella."

- A subhead that explains the value: "Join my VIP list and get the secret origin story that's not available anywhere else."
- A single field for their email address and a big damn button that says "Get the Free Book."

That should be the **first thing they see** when they land on your site. "Above the fold," as they say in the newspaper game. Right there in the hero section. No scrolling required.

Think of your homepage like a booth at a convention. You don't start the pitch with a three-minute bio. You start with: "Do you like sci-fi thrillers with killer AI?" Boom—engaged. Same logic applies here.

If your signup form isn't visible the second someone lands on your homepage without scrolling, then it might as well not be there.

Seriously.

This is called "above the fold" or "above the scroll." It's prime digital real estate. It's where attention lives. And if you bury your email opt-in below your bio, under a few book covers, or in your footer, you're just lighting opportunities on fire.

You need your **lead magnet** or **signup CTA** to be front and center, as in:

- Big headline: "Get a Free Book Today"
- One-sentence promise: "Join the VIP list and download the prequel novella instantly."
- Email field + big button: "Send My Freebie"

People don't scroll unless they're already interested. Your job is to make them interested *before* they scroll.

Put the opt-in in the hero section. Make it the first thing they see. Make it so obvious it feels weird *not* to sign up.

That's how you grow your list without begging.

YOUR HOMEPAGE SHOULD DO EXACTLY TWO THINGS

If you're trying to make your homepage do everything, it will do nothing well. Your homepage should answer these two questions instantly:

- **Who is this site for?** (What kind of reader will enjoy your work?)
- **What should I do next?** (And why should I care?)

Here's what that means in practice:

- A clean headline that says what you write and why it matters. Something like: "Heart-pounding fantasy thrillers for readers who miss old-school adventure."
- A visual cue like a book cover or box set that signals the genre immediately.
- One or two buttons max. One should be your lead magnet. The other, if you must, can be "Shop Books" or "Start the Series." That's it. No more than two.

You are not Amazon. You don't need to list your entire bibliography on the homepage. Link to a store or books page for that. Here, your job is to keep the reader's focus tight.

STRIP THE MENU TO THE BONES

Most author sites look like someone vomited a sitemap all over the top bar. Stop doing that.

You don't need twelve links. You don't need "Media Kit" or "Appearances" or "Gallery" unless you're actively booking gigs or selling photography. Cut it down to the essentials:

- Home
- Books (or Store)
- About
- Contact

If you have a lead magnet, add a link for it: "Free Book" or "VIP Club." If you're primarily driving newsletter signups, make that the standout link. Use a different color or button style so it catches the eye.

This isn't about minimalism for aesthetics, it's about reducing decisions. Fewer choices = faster conversions.

HIGHLIGHT JUST ONE BOOK OR SERIES

If your homepage is your storefront window, don't fill it with everything you've ever made. Feature your strongest or most relevant product.

That usually means:

- Your latest release
- The first book in your bestselling series
- A discounted box set

You should include:

- A 3D image of the cover or boxed set
- A snappy blurb or reader quote (1–2 lines)
- A "Buy Now" or "Learn More" button that leads to the sales page

This reinforces genre, adds social proof, and gives the reader a clear path to purchase if they're ready. It also gives you flexibility: if your CTA is "join the list," then this featured book helps warm up that lead.

ADD ONE LINE ABOUT YOU (NOT A BIO!)

Readers like to know there's a human behind the site. But they don't need your whole backstory here.

Write a single line under your signup or feature section like:

"I'm Jordan Cole, an indie author obsessed with magical conspiracies and broken heroes."

Include a small photo if you want. Link to your full About page if they're curious. But don't waste prime homepage space on a three-paragraph life story.

USE TRUST BUILDERS WISELY

You want your homepage to do emotional work:

- Reassure readers they're in the right place.
- Remove doubt about the quality of your work.

That means strategically adding elements like:

- A single strong review quote: "One of the best books I've read this year. – ★★★★★ Goodreads reviewer"
- A short badge section if you have them: "USA Today Bestseller" or "As Seen In…" logos
- Mention your reader base: "Over 10,000 readers and counting."

Keep these small and tight. One good quote. One or two credibility markers. That's all you need.

DON'T FORGET THE FOOTER

It's boring, but necessary:

- Include links to Privacy Policy and Terms.

- Add social icons (if you actually use social media).
- You can repeat your main CTA—email signup or book link—here too.

And make sure it looks like the rest of your site. Cohesive branding matters more than people admit.

YOUR HOMEPAGE ISN'T STATIC

The most powerful homepage is one that evolves.

- Test your headline. Try different wordings.
- Swap out the lead magnet title.
- Move your signup higher.
- Watch user behavior with free tools like Hotjar or Microsoft Clarity.

Your homepage should change as your strategy evolves. New book? New freebie? New offer? Update the damn site. Don't let it rot.

If you're going to sell direct, your homepage isn't just part of the brand. **It is *the* brand.**

And now that yours is dialed in, we can move on to the second most important page on your site: your store.

YOUR WEBSTORE IS A SALES ENGINE, NOT A CATALOG

The biggest mistake authors make when they start selling direct is that they think their store should look like a miniature Amazon.

So, they list every book they've ever written, slap a "buy" button under each one, and call it a day. No bundles. No urgency. No point of view.

That's not a store. That's a spreadsheet.

If you want to make real money selling direct, your store needs to do more than display your work. It needs to **move people through an experience** where *you* control the pricing, the framing, the flow, and the outcome.

The key to that is **unique bundles**.

When someone shops on Amazon, they're looking for the lowest price, the fastest shipping, or the next book in the series. You can't out-Amazon Amazon. So, stop trying.

Your superpower as a direct seller is **exclusivity**. You can create things Amazon never will like book + print bundles, digital box sets with bonus stories, signed limited editions, launch-only merch, or seasonal "mystery reader boxes" with art cards, maps, stickers, whatever fits your brand.

These aren't just "things to sell." They're reasons to buy from you instead of anywhere else.

Because here's the truth: people don't go to author websites to pay full price for the same thing they could get cheaper on Kindle. They go because they want something *more*.

BUNDLES MAKE ADS SCALE

You know what doesn't scale well? Running a $10 Facebook ad to sell a $2.99 ebook.

You'll burn your money fast, and at best, break even.

But when you have a $40 digital bundle with five books and exclusive bonuses? Now you've got margin. Now you've got room to spend $5, $10, even $15 to acquire a customer and still make a profit.

Bundles aren't just cool. They're **strategic**.

They give you the room to test copy. To experiment with audiences. To build retargeting funnels. They make your marketing sustainable.

And if you add urgency with limited stock, time-sensitive offers, or bonuses that expire, you create a reason to buy *right now* instead of "maybe someday."

STOREFRONT AS A LAUNCH PAD

Think of your webstore as your personal con booth, except it's open 24/7 and reaches the whole planet.

Would you set up a table with every book you've ever written and just sit there silently, hoping someone gets it? No. You'd pitch your best thing. You'd bundle your series. You'd highlight what's new. You'd offer show specials.

Your store should do the same.

Every quarter, swap in new bundles. Every season, roll out a themed offer. Every time you launch, build a special edition that's only available direct.

You're not just building a storefront. You're building a destination where your readers check in with because they know cool stuff lives there.

And when you do it right, you stop being "just another author" and start becoming their author.

LANDING PAGES THAT DON'T SUCK

If your homepage is your handshake and your store is your shop window, then your landing pages are your pitch room. It's where you drive someone to take a single, very specific action, and where distractions go to die.

Landing pages are focused. They're stripped down. They don't try to do five things at once. And that's what makes them so damn powerful.

They need to revolve around One Offer, One Page, Zero Distractions

If it does not further the sale of that offer, strip it out.

When someone lands on your landing page, you've got maybe five seconds before they click away. That's it. That's the game.

Which means you don't have time to meander, warm them up, or slowly explain what you're offering. You have to grab them immediately with something specific, valuable, and, ideally, exclusive.

That starts with a bold headline. Not a clever one. A clear one.

"Get the complete 5-book bundle for 40% off—this week only."

That's a reason to care. A reason to read the next sentence. A reason to keep scrolling.

Under that, you need a gorgeous visual that reinforces the offer. A box set mockup, an art card preview, a signed hardcover photo, or whatever makes it feel real and valuable. Bonus points if it's something they can't get anywhere else.

And then you need one big, obvious button that says exactly what they should do: "Get the Bundle Now."

"Download Your Bonus." "Claim My Copy." None of this "Learn More" garbage.

That's all you want in the hero section. Not a menu bar. Not footer links. Not five different CTAs or a bunch of cross-sell junk. Focus is the whole point. You're guiding them down a funnel, not giving them a buffet.

MAKE THE OFFER SO OBVIOUS THEY CAN'T MISS IT

If someone has to scroll to understand what they're getting, you've already lost.

Spell it out immediately:

- What it is
- What's included
- Why it matters

Don't try to be coy. Don't bury the bonus chapter reveal halfway down the page. Don't assume they'll infer the value. Tell them.

"Instant download. Signed edition. Free map poster. Exclusive to this page."

And here's where the magic of urgency kicks into high gear.

People don't take action unless they think they'll miss out. So give them a real reason to move now.

Put a countdown timer on the offer. Say "Only 50 bundles available." Add "Offer ends Sunday at midnight."

You're not lying. You're setting boundaries. And those boundaries make the deal feel real.

Because it is real.

You're not Amazon. You don't have infinite copies. You're a creator running a limited-time experience. Let the reader feel that. Let it add weight to their decision.

And once they click, reward them. Make the delivery process smooth, the confirmation page fun, and the follow-up emails delightful.

Because this isn't just a sale. It's a trust transfer. And if you do it right, they'll come back.

BUILD TRUST AT THE BOTTOM

Right before someone buys, they'll look for reassurance. Give it to them:

- Secure checkout badges
- Refund policy
- Short FAQ with questions like "How will I receive my files?" or "Can I gift this to a friend?"

You don't need a wall of text. Just enough to smooth over objections.

So, your landing page should:

- Hook the reader with a bold headline.
- Reinforce value with copy and visuals.
- Guide them to one clear button.
- Remove hesitation with FAQs and trust signals.

If you do it right, they won't even notice how guided they feel. They'll just click.

And once they do—you've got them in your ecosystem, which is where the real magic happens.

THIS IS THE WORK THAT PAYS OFF FOREVER

Most authors treat their website like a checkbox. Something to get out of the way. Something that "looks professional." They obsess over the color scheme, stress about fonts, maybe even write a nice About page—and then leave it to rot for the next five years.

But not you. Not if you're serious. When you build your homepage to convert, when your store actually sells, and when your landing pages guide people to a clear yes— you're doing more than making a sale. You're building a system that works *even when you don't.*

This is the part of your business that compounds. Every new visitor has a place to land. Every new reader has a reason to stay. Every new offer has a stage.

It's not flashy. It's not fun. It's not sexy. But it's the spine that holds everything else together.

So invest the time. Get it right. And then watch what happens when your website starts doing its damn job. Your ads work better. Your launches get bigger. Your list grows on autopilot. Your store becomes a machine.

That's not magic. That's intentional design.

And now, you've got it.

HOW TO SUPERCHARGE YOUR WRITING CAREER WITH KICKSTARTER

If you're serious about building a direct sales business, Kickstarter isn't a "maybe." It's an integral part of your author career.

It's a launch strategy. It's a direct sales platform. It's a testing lab. It's a chance to validate your idea, connect with your readers, and fund your next creative leap without giving up control, rights, or royalties.

In my world, Kickstarter isn't just a tool I use once in a while. It's a foundational piece of how I build momentum, test offers, build out my product line, and get paid to develop new work.

I've launched campaigns that made almost nothing and ones that made over $45,000. And every single one of them helped me get better. Helped me reach more readers. Helped me build a deeper, more loyal audience.

This section is going to break down exactly how I do it: how to design smart rewards, how to structure your page, how to film a great video (without losing your mind), and how to treat each campaign like the experiment it is.

Because if you use Kickstarter right, it becomes the most powerful sales platform in your business.

VALIDATING YOUR IDEA...

Validating an idea is an essential component of any Kickstarter campaign, as it will tell you exactly how big your market is, and whether there is rabid interest, mild interest, or no interest in your product.

I always start my validation tests at **Google**, by typing in several keywords into the search engine and seeing how many results pop up. Google will tell you the sheer volume of terms related to your search. The higher, the better.

You can also run this search by going to the Google Adwords Keyword Planner, and typing in your search terms to get an idea of how active and popular your search terms are with people around the world.

Then I head over to Amazon and check the rankings of products. Again, I type in some similar search terms to what I'm trying to create.

Then, I click on the most popular products and see their popularity index on Amazon as a whole.

After that, I'll know exactly how popular the product is, how likely I am to find an audience, and roughly how much I can expect to raise from on Kickstarter.

Finally, I will run similar searches on Kickstarter and Indiegogo to see what hot topics there are in my category.

By doing this very quick search at the beginning, I will see if somebody has already created my idea. If so, I would abandon it in most cases.

None of the above are guarantees though. Just because there are no searches on Amazon or Google that return what you are trying to create, it's not necessarily a bust. It just means you'll have a longer row to hoe.

FINDING YOUR IDEAL AUDIENCE...

Finding your target market, and growing it, is the best predictor of how much money you are going to raise during your campaign.

Most people think they are going to click the launch button and magic is going to happen, but that's just not the case. It's a lot of hard work finding, building, and nurturing your audience.

However, if you find your target market, they will tell you exactly what they need and how to build a product that suits them. They are going to be your best beta testers and your best brand ambassadors.

They are not hard to find either.

I start finding an audience before I ever leave the house by joining Reddit forums and Facebook groups.

I join early and provide relevant comments and links to the members. I engage with them and find out what they are about. I truly care about what's going on, not just as a marketing gimmick.

Then, I leave my house by finding Meetup groups in my area.

While there may not be an audience for the exact product I'm trying to build near me, there is usually a group in the broad range of product class (i.e. if I'm trying to build a motorcycle motor, there is a motorcycle club even though it doesn't specialize in repair).

I join these groups a long time before I finish my product, provide updates, find friends, and talk shop. Then, when my product launches, I KNOW people want it because I have a community of hundreds of people that told me they want the product.

THE BEST TIME TO LAUNCH...

Finding the best time to launch is one of the biggest challenges with Kickstarter. There are several factors to consider, which all starts with the time of year.

Here's the truth: launching a Kickstarter after Thanksgiving or when school isn't in session is usually a bad idea.

Why?

Well during the summer people tend to be on vacation, so they are less present around their computer.

During the holidays, people are thinking about spending disposable income on gifts for people *not* a product they won't be getting until 4-6 months down the line.

Also, during the holidays you are competing with rock-bottom pricing from Amazon and other retailers.

Another traditionally bad time to launch would be right around tax time, because everybody has a tax bill due so the last thing they are thinking about is purchasing new stuff.

On the flip side, right after tax season when people are flush with cash is a great time to launch a product because most people have disposable income at that point.

But that's just one factor that goes into picking the right time. Another factor is buyer mentality. You want to hit a buyer with a product when it's hot in their mind.

The Coolest Cooler was one of the biggest Kickstarters ever, and the creator launched his product in June (which goes against what I just said and proves there are no rules in business) when people were thinking about summertime activities.

However, did you know that he also tried launching the same product the previous December to disastrous results?

There are many contributing factors to that, but most experts attribute this to the idea that nobody was thinking about, or cared about coolers, in December, so nobody bought it.

Another factor is your convention season. Every industry has conventions, and it's generally not the best idea to launch a Kickstarter during the biggest conventions because every big company is making announcements during CES and other shows.

While I do love having conventions as part of your launch strategy, I recommend smaller conventions where big companies aren't launching competing products.

There's just no way to compete with Samsung and Apple. They will destroy you.

The last factor I consider is backer psychology. People buy more when they are depressed.

People are the most depressed during the early months of the year, less so during the summer and around holidays, then there is another uptick around Labor Day until Halloween.

If I had to pin the best time down, I would say right after the New Year until March, and September-October as long as you can deliver by Christmas, are great times to launch.

However, it may be different in your industry and it's important to check for yourself using the factors we discussed

THE MOST IMPORTANT PART...

Ninety-nine percent of successful Kickstarter backer and pledge curves are the same. They are parabolas, with the beginning and end accounting for most of the backers and money raised.

You can see this by checking out campaigns on Kicktraq.

As you'll see, there will *always* be a lull in the middle of a campaign where you only have a couple of people backing a day.

I've only seen a couple of campaigns that were able to maintain momentum the entire campaign.

If we accept that as fact, then the most important part of the Kickstarter is building for a HUGE release on the first day.

Seriously.

You need to raise 33% of your backing on the first day. If you can do that, you're nearly guaranteed to succeed. If you can't, your path will be much harder. If you fall below 20% on your first day, you're in for a very long, expensive haul to get your project funded.

Having a fantastic first day means so much.

It means that your backers are going to be spreading the word about your campaign throughout your campaign. That's a lot of free publicity.

Additionally, it means you will show up higher on Kickstarter, you have a better chance of people seeing your campaign, and when they see your campaign, they see it as a success.

People love to back a winner. If you can hit that 33% mark on the first day, people will want to back your campaign because success breeds more success.

Additionally, the higher your backers are at the beginning, the more people will back during the middle of your campaign. The higher your first day, the higher the minimum pledges will be in future days.

So finding those backers on day one, and telling people about the campaign, and getting as many people to back as possible is critical and you need to start early to do it. The bigger your network, the bigger your reach, and the more people you can hit on that first day.

CREATING YOUR CAMPAIGN FOR MAXIMUM IMPACT...

Creating a Kickstarter campaign comes down to three sections: the video, the copy, and the rewards.

First and foremost, you should have a video. Almost 70% of Kickstarters without videos fail. That means if you don't have a campaign video, you only have a 30% chance of succeeding.

Additionally, people want to see you in the video, because they are buying you as much as your product. On Kickstarter, you and your product are intrinsically linked.

There's a really simple strategy for making a video in three steps.

- *Introduction* of no more than 15 seconds.
- **A product demo** where you show the coolness of the product for no more than a minute.
- Coming back on camera and *making a case for your project* for no more than another minute where you talk about the history of the product and why you need backing.

Total run time should be no more than 2:30! That's two minutes and thirty seconds, not two hours. Keep it short. I've used this on all my campaigns, and it works really well, especially for books. People want to connect with the author.

The second part is the campaign copy.

Make sure to break up sections into easily digestible tidbits. Assume people are going to fall off while reading it. Therefore, put the coolest thing about your project at the top accompanied by an awesome image, then break up sections throughout the campaign to show off your product.

Remember, this is a marketing piece, not a short story. Nobody wants to read big paragraphs. They also don't want to wonder what you are talking about. If it doesn't keep them interested, they will click off.

The final bit is the rewards. Rewards need to be simple, concise, and explain explicitly what people get for their pledge. They do not need fancy names, just clear concise information. Each of your rewards has a purpose and should be targeted at a specific buyer profile.

DISTRIBUTING YOUR CAMPAIGN WITHOUT BREAKING THE BANK

Once your campaign is over, we have to talk about getting your campaign into backer hands. This is where most Kickstarters go bankrupt...or at least end up massively in the red. That's exactly why budgeting appropriately is so important.

Getting a high-quality project into backers' hands is the best way to build an audience for the future, and that's the goal of Kickstarter.

Funding the project is a part of Kickstarter, but it's only a part. Your goal should be building an audience so you can keep doing Kickstarters forever.

In order to do that you need to precisely know how much it will cost to get your project into backer hands, who is going to produce your project, how you are going to distribute it, how you are going to ship it, and build in contingencies. This needs to happen before you hit the launch button.

You need quotes from your fulfillment, distribution, and shipping companies before you launch, and at different levels depending on how many people back.

Additionally, you have to keep your audience updated on everything, both good and bad. Here's the thing. In order to build an audience, you have to communicate with your audience, be honest with them, and get them their project in a timely manner.

BUILDING FOR THE FUTURE...

When you're talking about building for the future, you should do everything in your power to make people say WOW. Once they are wowed by your professionalism and quality, they are very likely to back again.

Now, once you finish your Kickstarter the first thing you need to do is find an email program like MailChimp, Mailblast, or Flodesk and start communication with your backers on at least a monthly basis. Do not wait until your next project to keep people informed. They will forget about you.

Then, you need to start planning your next project. You are no longer a hobbyist. Once you finish your campaign and start to launch your next, you are a business. However, you can't really go full force until after backers get their rewards.

KICKSTARTER IS A LAUNCHPAD, NOT A LIFELINE

One of the biggest mistakes authors make with Kickstarter is treating it like a glorified pre-order. They show up with the same offer, the same copy, the same assumptions they were going to use for retail, and hope it works.

But Kickstarter isn't a mirror of your retail launch. It's a microscope. It's where you figure out whether your pitch actually lands before you throw real money at it.

This is the part of the process that separates career authors from hopeful ones: we don't guess what will work. We test it live.

When I say "testing ground," I don't mean you slap a campaign together and see what sticks. I mean you use Kickstarter to pressure-test every part of your launch— from your offer structure to your messaging to your product line. You're not just launching a book. You're collecting intel.

- If your $25 hardcover tier outperforms the $10 ebook tier by 3 to 1? That's data.
- If your "everything bundle" pulls 40% of your total revenue? That's a signal.

- If three backers email you about an idea you *didn't* offer, guess what? You just uncovered a product gap.

Kickstarter gives you something Amazon never will: direct customer feedback tied to actual buying behavior. Not clicks. Not guesses. Actual dollars.

And ***every single element*** of your Kickstarter can be repurposed.

- The copy that converts on your campaign page becomes your sales page.
- The reward tier structure becomes your bundle strategy on your store.
- The email sequences that drove pledges become evergreen onboarding automations.

You get paid to test your marketing in public, with warm leads, before you ever run an ad.

You can't do that with a webstore. You can't do that with Amazon. Kickstarter gives you a live environment with low risk, high insight, and enough margin to actually make mistakes and still come out ahead.

So, stop treating it like a one-and-done launch. Start treating it like the lab where you build the next phase of your business.

Because if you use it well, Kickstarter isn't the end of the funnel. It's the blueprint.

THE BASICS MOST PEOPLE GET WRONG

Kickstarter is not your boss. It's not your publisher. It's not your last-ditch chance to make a book happen. It's just a platform—a powerful one—but only if you treat it with the right mindset.

Most creators walk into Kickstarter hoping it'll save them, but Kickstarter doesn't save you. It reflects you. It reflects how much trust you've built, how good your offer is, and how clearly you've communicated it.

So, before we get to the fancy parts, you have to understand what the platform actually is: **a way to test and sell new products to your warmest audience**.

Let's break that down:

KICKSTARTER IS A TEST

Every campaign is a mini-market launch. You're not just asking "Will people buy this?"—you're answering *how* they'll buy it, *which formats* they want, and *how much* they're willing to spend.

Use Kickstarter to:

- Test pricing (does the $40 tier outperform the $25?)
- Test cover options (mock up two versions and see which drives pledges)
- Test bundling strategies (ebooks + merch vs. digital-only)
- Test messaging (change your story headline mid-campaign and see if conversions shift)

This is your sandbox. It's a way to de-risk bigger launches by putting ideas in front of your most engaged fans *first*.

KICKSTARTER IS SALES, NOT DISCOVERABILITY

You are the traffic. You are the engine. You cannot count on Kickstarter to bring you backers. Their organic discovery is real, but it only works **after** you've proven momentum. That means email list, social posts, ads, podcasts, direct messages, whatever you've got.

Think of it like a pop-up store. Kickstarter handles the checkout counter. You're in charge of getting people in the door.

The biggest predictor of campaign success? How fast you fund. Hitting 30% in the first 48 hours sets you up for the algorithm to take notice. That means:

- Build your list *before* launch.
- Warm them up *before* you launch.
- Stack your audience to show up *right when* it goes live.

You need urgency. Not desperation. Not a guilt trip. Just a well-timed push.

And once you've funded? Then you can start playing. Then you add stretch goals. You stack upgrades. You message backers. You turn that early success into a snowball.

KICKSTARTER IS THE START OF THE RELATIONSHIP

Not everyone who backs your campaign will stick around. But a lot of them will *if you onboard them properly.*

- Deliver fast.
- Communicate often.
- Offer a next step: mailing list, store link, future launch.

The backer isn't the end of the sale. They're the beginning of a reader journey. Treat them like gold. Because if you do? They'll show up again. And again. And again.

That's the mindset. That's the foundation.

Now let's dig into the rewards—the part where you actually make your money.

MINE THE PUBLIC DATA GOLDMINE

Every Kickstarter campaign is a fully transparent case study sitting in plain sight. Click on any campaign, successful or not, live or archived, and you can see things like how many backers pledged, which reward tiers they chose, what they spent, and exactly when momentum spiked or stalled. Pair that with free tracking tools like Kicktraq or BiggerCake and you can export pledge curves, average pledge values, and backer-count velocity for any project in any genre, no scraping required.

- **Reverse-engineer winning rewards.** Sort a successful campaign's reward table by popularity: note the price breaks, format mixes (digital-only, print, deluxe), and how each tier nudges buyers to climb the value ladder. Do the same for under-performers to see where complexity, poor pricing, or irrelevant add-ons killed conversion, then adjust your own ladder accordingly.
- **Study update cadence and content.** Mine the updates and plot which posts coincide with pledge spikes. You'll quickly spot patterns that reignite momentum. Borrow the cadence, not the copy: match their rhythm to your voice and audience size.
- **Time your launch window.** Kicktraq's daily breakdown shows which weekdays and hours deliver the highest pledge velocity in your niche. If the top three campaigns in your genre all funded 30% on a Tuesday morning, you have a data-backed clue for your own Day-One blast.
- **Benchmark realistic goals.** Filter campaigns by category and funding level, then average the top ten. You'll know whether a $10K ask is ambitious or conservative for a 300-page fantasy hardcover and you

can price rewards to hit that number without guesswork.

Treat Kickstarter like a public lab notebook: every success and flop is open-source intelligence. Spend an afternoon dissecting campaigns before you build your own and you'll skip months of trial and error—launching with data-driven confidence instead of hopeful hunches.

REWARDS THAT ACTUALLY SELL

The rewards section is where most Kickstarter campaigns live or die. Because this isn't just a tip jar. You're not hoping someone tosses you five bucks out of pity. You're selling a product—and every single tier you offer is a chance to move someone further into your world.

That means every reward tier needs to do two things:

- Make sense on its own.
- Make the next one up look even better.

This is what I call a value ladder. And if you build it right, backers will climb it without hesitation.

Start simple. Offer a digital-only tier that's clear and clean. Then build from there: paperback, hardcover, bundles, collector editions, deluxe boxes. Don't just pile on extra stuff. Give each level a *reason* to exist.

And make sure your rewards match the kind of backers you want to attract. If you want super fans to drop $100+, then you better offer something they can't get anywhere else—signed books, personalized swag, exclusive extras.

At the same time, don't forget your impulse buyers. The $1 "just support" tier can bring in hundreds of people who wouldn't have backed otherwise—but who might buy something later. That's not just padding your backer count. That's long-term strategy.

Most important of all: **every reward tier must be easy to understand.** No cryptic names. No inside jokes. Don't make backers do math or guess what's included. Spell it out. Use images. Repeat info if you need to.

Because here's the truth: confused people don't convert. And Kickstarter is a sales platform.

So make your rewards a no-brainer. Build the ladder. Show them how to climb it. And then make that top tier so good they can't help but jump in with both feet.

When I build rewards, I don't start with what I want to sell. I start with what kind of **experience** I want to offer.

- **Do I want this campaign to feel premium and limited?** Then I build toward deluxe bundles with prints, signed editions, and timed exclusives.
- **Do I want it to feel fast and digital?** Then I simplify everything to just ebooks, audiobooks, and digital bonuses.

I don't cram every format into every launch. That's how campaigns get bloated and confusing. Instead, I create **tracks**.

Maybe one track is for digital readers who just want the files, one for collectors who want the hardcovers, and one for super-backers who want the whole damn stack— books, merch, signed extras, bonus content, maybe a Zoom call.

That's the spine of the campaign. Then I build the value ladder inside each track.

For example, in a print track:

- **Tier 1:** Signed paperback of Book 1
- **Tier 2:** Paperback bundle of all 3 books
- **Tier 3:** Hardcover bundle with signed bookplates
- **Tier 4:** Collector's box with exclusive merch + early access bonus

Each step makes the next one look like a no-brainer. It's not about nickel-and-diming people, it's about giving them *a reason to upgrade*.

And here's where most creators miss it: **the top tiers matter more than you think**. Maybe only 2–5 people will grab the $150 or $250 tier—but they might bring in 25–30% of your revenue. That's why I always include a "get everything I've ever made" tier. Even if nobody bites, just having it there **pulls the rest of the campaign up**.

And I don't guess on prices. I base them on what has worked before, what my audience has actually paid in past campaigns, and what other campaigns can support. I look at the backer report from the last campaign and say, "Okay, 40 people picked the $50 bundle. Let's build from there."

I also price shipping into the tiers. No surprises. No backer drop-off. Just clear pricing, visible value, and emotional logic.

HOW WE TEST REWARDS

We don't guess. We launch, watch, and adapt.

When we're testing reward tiers, we're looking at **backer behavior in real time**. This means tracking *which tiers convert, when people back*, and *what patterns emerge over the first 48–72 hours*.

PRE-LAUNCH TESTING

Before the campaign goes live:

- **Look at previous campaigns**: What were the top 3 most-selected tiers last time? Start from there.
- **Ask your audience**: In your email list or social group, run a quick poll: "If I offered X, would you prefer A, B, or C?"
- **Use past performance as a forecast**: Did the $60 bundle dominate your last launch? Don't reinvent the wheel. Improve it.
- **Preview Page Feedback**: Send your Kickstarter preview page to 5–10 trusted readers and ask where they paused, got confused, or hesitated.

LIVE TESTING (ONCE THE CAMPAIGN LAUNCHES)

- **Watch pledge velocity**: If Tier 3 stalls while Tier 2 and Tier 4 move, that's a sign Tier 3 needs a clearer value bump or repositioning.
- **Create urgency with mid-campaign bonuses**: Add "early bird ends tonight" or "bonus art print added to all $40+ tiers this week" to test how people respond to FOMO.
- **Run an update with a new offer**: "Hey, we're adding a new $75 tier that includes all three hardcovers and the limited-edition sticker pack." Then watch what happens over 24 hours.
- **Message backers** who chose the $1 tier and ask what held them back. Sometimes you'll get product gold from their answers.
- **You can't delete a tier once somebody backs it,** but you can sunset it so that it gets buried at the end of the rewards.

POST-CAMPAIGN REVIEW

- Sort your backer report by revenue and tier.
- Highlight:
    - Which tiers overperformed?
    - Where did most people drop off?
    - Did expensive tiers bring in the volume—or just big numbers from a few whales?

This isn't just analysis, it's planning for the *next* launch. What worked once usually works again. But don't assume anything. Use your last campaign to sharpen your next one.

Kickstarter is a laboratory. Every tier is an experiment. The good news? The results come with receipts.

THE PAGE IS THE PITCH

Your Kickstarter page is not a press release. It's not a Wikipedia entry. It's not a blog post. It's a **sales page**, and if you don't treat it like one, you're leaving money on the table.

This is where the real persuasion happens. Your video hooks them, your rewards tempt them, but the story section? That's what converts them.

It's where you make the emotional argument. It's where you say, "Here's what this is, here's why it matters, and here's why now."

And yes, it's also where you lay out what's included, what the tiers mean, and why your backers should trust you to deliver.

Let's break it down.

START WITH ALIGNMENT

You want your reader to nod along before they've even seen a reward.

That means starting with a few emotional yeses. "Do you love morally gray heroes? Are you craving a new epic fantasy with a heavy dose of political intrigue?" Those are mini-commitments. And if someone says yes to those, they're already halfway to pledging.

Then, give them the vibe. One paragraph max. What is this book or series? Not the plot. The pitch. The feeling. Why it's exciting.

"This is a brutal, high-octane revenge story for fans of John Wick, Brandon Sanderson, and ancient Greek mythology."

Boom. Now they know where they are.

CLEAR BEATS CLEVER EVERY TIME

There's this persistent myth among writers—especially writers who fancy themselves wordsmiths—that the goal of a sales page is to be clever. To dazzle. To prove you're interesting.

It's not.

The goal of your Kickstarter page is to **convert**. That means clarity trumps cleverness every time.

You might love your reward names like "The Hero's Journey" or "The Dungeon Master's Hoard," but if a reader doesn't immediately know whether that means *ebook, paperback,* or *limited edition hardback with stickers and a map*…they're going to freeze. And when people freeze, they leave.

You've got about five seconds to show people exactly what they're getting—and why they should want it. That's it.

So instead of The Sorcerer's Secret say:

The Complete Hardcover Box Set – Signed + Bonus Map

Instead of The Bard's Ballad say Digital Bundle – All 3 Books + Audiobook + Bonus Chapter

It might not make your inner poet sing, but it makes your *backer's brain* relax. They don't have to think. They don't have to decode. They can just say, "Hell yes, that's what I want."

Same goes for your page headers. Don't write "A Journey Begins…" when you mean "What You Get." Don't label your CTA "Join the Fight" if you're trying to get people to back your campaign. Just say:

"Back this Project and Get Your Bundle"

Be clever *inside* the product. Be crystal clear on the sales page.

Because when clarity wins, you do too.

SHOW, DON'T JUST SAY

Mockups matter. Visuals matter. You want the book to feel real in their hands. You want the bonuses to feel tactile. Use 3D covers. Show stacks. Preview prints or stretch goal upgrades. Make the offer feel like something they can't get anywhere else.

And explain what's inside: 300 pages, full-color interiors, signed hardcover, printed maps—whatever you're offering. Make it specific. Make it tangible.

ANSWER THEIR QUESTIONS BEFORE THEY ASK

Your page should build trust with every scroll.

- Is the book done? Say so.
- How's it being printed? Tell them.
- When will it ship? Be honest.
- What happens if you hit stretch goals? Explain it.

Add a section for "Where is the money going?" even if your only answer is "printing, shipping, and covering production." Transparency builds loyalty.

GUIDE THE FLOW

Organize your story page like a funnel:

- **Hook (headline, vibe):** This is the emotional opening. The goal is immediate alignment. You want readers to say "Yes, this is for me" within five seconds. The hook includes a bold headline and a short pitch that sets the tone—genre, stakes, voice. Think vibe over plot: "An epic fantasy revenge saga for fans of Sanderson and John Wick." That's the first yes.
- **Offer (mockups, summary):** This is where you show the thing you're selling. Physical books? Art prints? Collector boxes? Use 3D mockups, lifestyle shots, and short copy that makes the reward tangible. This is the "you get this" part of the sales page. It's where desire gets anchored in reality.
- **Details (format, bonuses, stretch goals):** Now we drill down. What's in the book? Hardcover or

paperback? Is it signed? How many pages? What format is the digital version? What happens if we hit $5k? $10k? This section answers questions for serious buyers who want to know exactly what they're getting—and what they *might* get if the campaign takes off.

- **Trust (who you are, what you've done):** Backers want to know who's behind the curtain. This doesn't need to be your life story, just a few lines about you as a creator, what else you've made, and your experience running or fulfilling campaigns. Include review quotes, credibility signals, or audience size if relevant. This is the "why should I believe you?" part of the page.

- **Logistics (shipping, timeline, fulfillment plan):** This is where the buyer brain kicks in. When will it arrive? How is it getting made? Will it be printed overseas? Are you using a fulfillment partner? Be upfront. Even if you're still figuring things out, share what you *do* know and be transparent. It turns hesitation into trust.

- **CTA (encouragement to back now):** End with momentum. Tell them what to do. This isn't a soft "thanks for reading"—it's a confident call-to-action: "If you love epic fantasy and want a signed first edition with exclusive extras, this is the time. Back now and join the rebellion." Make it feel urgent. Make it feel personal.

And remember: don't just dump info. *Curate* it.

THE VIDEO IS YOUR 120-SECOND HANDSHAKE

You don't need a film crew. You need honesty, energy, and a clear promise.

Here's the formula:

- Start with your face. Introduce yourself. "Hey, I'm [name], and I write books about [hook]."
- Pitch the series like you would at a convention.
- Show some visuals—covers, mockups, maybe a stack of books on your desk.
- Ask for the pledge. "If this sounds like your kind of story, I'd love your support."

Keep it under two minutes. Under one, if you can swing it. The goal is *not* to tell the whole story. It's to get them to keep reading.

Authenticity beats polish. Always.

Your video and page work together. One sells the story. One closes the deal.

Now that you've nailed your pitch and your rewards, let's make sure the whole thing performs when it hits the real world. Next up: launch strategy, stretch goals, and what to do when things go sideways.

STRATEGY IS THE WHOLE GAME

People think Kickstarter success is about having the best product or the prettiest video or the most polished rewards.

It's not.

Success lives or dies in your **strategy**. And strategy is just a fancy way of saying: how do you keep momentum moving from Day One to Day Thirty without burning out or making your audience hate you?

That's what this chapter is about.

It's the stuff you don't see on the campaign page. It's the prep, the pacing, the structure behind the show. And it's the reason some campaigns raise $20,000 and others sputter out at $1,500 even with similar products.

Let's talk about how we build a strategy that performs.

WEEKLY PERKS ARE MARKETING PACING, NOT FAN SERVICE

One of the biggest misconceptions I see is this idea that weekly perks—those stretch goals, bonuses, reveals, new tiers—are just fun little surprises for your backers.

They're not. They're pacing mechanisms.

They're how you break up a 30-day campaign into something that feels active instead of exhausting. Something that has a pulse instead of a flatline.

Every week, you need a beat. A reason to post. A reason to update. A reason to re-engage people who already backed and give the fence-sitters something new to say yes to.

This is how you build campaign rhythm:

- **Week 1:** Early bird bonus ends Friday
- **Week 2:** Backer goal unlocks new reward
- **Week 3:** Surprise add-on or new merch tier
- **Week 4:** Final push bonus, countdown bundle, all-in tier

Each move is a marketing event, not a giveaway.

You're not handing out perks because you're generous. You're pacing your story. And your campaign is the story you're telling.

CAMPAIGN LENGTH = MARKETING LOAD

So, how long should your Kickstarter run?

The answer isn't about audience size. It's about **marketing stamina**.

If you're launching with five days of pre-written emails, two updates, and one graphic, then **a 30-day campaign will destroy you**. You'll run out of things to say by Week Two, and your energy will die before your deadline even shows up.

But if you've got:

- Weekly bonus content planned
- Mid-campaign perks queued up
- A warm list ready to back
- A visibility strategy across channels

Then a 30-day campaign gives you room to breathe, and room to scale.

Short campaigns are like sprints. Great when you've got high momentum and a hot list.

Long campaigns are marathons. Worth it if you've got enough water stations (aka content) along the way.

You can't just pick a date and hope it works out. You have to plan how you'll keep the engine running at every turn.

The perk isn't the point. The **engagement** is.

THE FIRST 48 HOURS ARE EVERYTHING

If you don't walk into launch day already 30% funded, you're fighting an uphill battle.

The algorithm isn't going to save you. "Kickstarter magic" isn't real. What is real? Intent.

I want a couple hundred people ready to click "Back this project" the second it goes live. That means I've been warming them up for 2–3 weeks with behind-the-scenes posts, early looks at rewards, teaser videos, polls, maybe even preview pages.

I don't hope for momentum. I build it.

Because if I can cross 100 backers on Day One, the Kickstarter discovery engine starts working, and more people start sharing about it, creating a positive feedback loop.

And if I hit 50% in the first few days? I can start playing offense. That's when stretch goals come into play.

STRETCH GOALS ARE STORY BEATS

A good stretch goal plan isn't just a list of rewards. It's a pacing strategy.

You're giving people a reason to care after they've already backed.

Think of them like episodic milestones. When we hit $5k, everyone gets a foil upgrade. At $7,500, you unlock a digital wallpaper set. At $10k, you get a brand-new bonus story.

And we don't dump them all at once. We reveal them as we go. That way, there's always a reason to check in again, to share the campaign, to bump up your pledge.

And don't forget backer goals. "When we hit 300 backers, everyone gets a bonus bookmark." That gets your community to spread the word for you. Because now it's not just about money, it's about momentum.

But stretch goals only work if you've priced your base campaign correctly. If you're counting on stretch goals to survive, you're already screwed.

You don't use them to save your campaign. You use them to scale it.

WELCOME TO THE DEAD ZONE

Every campaign hits it. Days 8–20 are just… slower. The launch rush fades, the final countdown hasn't started yet, and you're sitting there staring at a stalled graph wondering if it's over.

It's not over, but this is where you earn your paycheck.

Dead zones are where you inject **new energy** into the campaign. That could mean:

- Introducing a new bundle
- Dropping a mid-campaign bonus
- Adding a time-limited add-on
- Doing a stretch goal reveal
- Posting a creator update or backer Q&A

And you don't have to do it all at once. Drip it out. One move every few days to keep the wheel spinning.

Dead zones aren't death sentences. They're just **strategy gaps waiting to be filled**.

On a normal campaign, 1/3 of your raise will come in the first week, 1/3 in the dead zone, and 1/3 in the last week. If you don't have a strategy for the dead zone, you're missing 1/3 of the money you could raise.

CLOSE WITH CONFIDENCE

Most campaigns end the way they started, fast and chaotic. You want that. You want the final 72 hours to feel like a launch all over again.

Here's how we do it:

- Schedule reminder emails for anyone who's followed but not pledged.
- Hit your list again: "Last chance for the exclusive bundle."
- Add a final-day-only offer. Something clean and exciting.
- Post a heartfelt update thanking backers and setting up the final goal.

Make the last few days feel **personal and exciting**. Don't guilt people. Don't panic. Just lead like a pro and trust your momentum.

Because here's the truth: backers remember how your campaign made them *feel*. And a strong finish leaves a better impression than a flashy start.

You can't see a great strategy from the outside. But you can feel it.

A good strategy makes your campaign feel inevitable. Like it was always going to win. Like the creator knew what they were doing and had their shit together.

That's what we're building.

This isn't a magic trick. It's just work. Smart, premeditated, paced work.

And now you've got the blueprint.

Russell Nohelty

30 KICKSTARTER TIPS TO HELP CRUSH YOUR CAMPAIGN GOALS

I've been running Kickstarter campaigns since 2014 and backing them since way before then. In fact, I just realized I joined Kickstarter all the way back in 2011, even though I didn't run my first project for 4 more years.

Since I started running campaigns, I've raised over $650,000 across over forty different campaigns from children's books, to novels, to comics, and worked with dozens of other creators on their campaigns.

Across all the years I've been working with Kickstarter, some common tips stand the test of time, and that is what I've compiled here.

TIP #1: START KICKSTARTER PLANNING EARLY

You should be building your audience for at least three months before you launch a campaign. You can't be successful in crowdfunding without a crowd.

That means showing off your project, starting a Facebook group, beefing up your social media presence, making press contacts, and building a newsletter.

The more time you have to build your network and prep them for a Kickstarter project that's coming, the more likely they will be to back your campaign when it's time.

TIP #2: SEND INDIVIDUAL THANK YOU NOTES TO BACKERS

When somebody gives you their hard earned money, it is only polite to say thank you. It's easy for us to treat our backers as money, but they are humans and adding the human touch will improve your connection.

On top of being the right thing to do, it will also stem the loss of backers toward the middle of your campaign because you are making a connection.

TIP #3: STRETCH GOALS SHOULD ALWAYS MAKE YOUR CORE KICKSTARTER PRODUCT BETTER

Most people have terrible trouble with stretch goals. Once a project funds the backers fall off because there's nothing more to keep their interest.

You can change that by making sure your stretch goals always improve the quality of your project. For instance, if you have a book that is a 100-page softcover comic, you can add extra pages at the end as a stretch goal, you can add an extra story, you can make your soft cover a hardcover, you could make your book a bigger size.

Meanwhile, the original backer is still paying the same amount for their pledge, and they are getting a better product. Nobody cares about the bookmarks and prints. They just want the coolest project they can get.

TIP #4: KEEP YOUR KICKSTARTER REWARDS SIMPLE

There is no need to add multiple options for similar items. Each reward should be targeting a specific buyer and have enough space in between to clearly delineate the right buyer for that product.

I recommend you start with a $1, $10, $25, $50, and $250 for a standard book. Obviously, certain products will not fall into this range, but for a publishing product, these five categories should be your base. You can always add later.

TIP #5: MAKE DEPOSITS INTO THE KICKSTARTER GOODWILL BANK

Goodwill is a finite resource, and you will use it up when you run a campaign. In order to make running a Kickstarter palatable to your audience, you need to add value to people's lives for months and months before you ask them to pledge to your campaign.

This could be from a web-comic, or free pages from your book, or a podcast helping them fix their biggest problems, or anything you can do to help add value to your audience's lives. The more value you add, the more trust you will have with your audience and the fuller your goodwill bank will become.

TIP #6: DON'T OVEREXTEND YOURSELF ON MERCHANDISE

Especially once a project is funded, creators generally go crazy offering all sorts of merchandise like t-shirts, mugs, and other very high-priced items. The problem is that they are eating into their own profit margins and eventually end up in the red.

Merchandise is unnecessary in almost all instances until you have a well-known product. Just focus on making a great single product (unless your product is incredibly high-priced like many tech products are). If you must make merchandise, don't make anything with multiple sizes. Also note that if you offer merchandise you can no longer ship your product media mail.

TIP #7: KEEP YOUR VIDEO UNDER THREE MINUTES

Your video is a commercial, and nobody can stand a commercial for more than a couple minutes, no matter how amazing the commercial. You can say everything you need to say in under three minutes.

Yes, you will have to edit yourself down. There are plenty of free programs like iMovie, which can take out all the ums and ah. You need to make your case clearly and succinctly, so people don't tune out.

TIP #8: ADD LOTS OF IMAGES

The average successful Kickstarter has 11 images in it. Even if you have something with a novel, there are plenty of images you can add besides your cover. You can add a photo of yourself. You can add some quotes from your book overlaid on top of a royalty free image. You can add silly memes. You can have somebody draw some illustrations of your book.

In whatever the case, your book needs images. Humans are visual creatures and pictures help improve the quality of your page and make your project look more professional.

TIP #9: KEEP YOUR TEXT CONCISE

People on Kickstarter love to use huge blocks of text, but that is ugly to the eye. They also love to muddle their paragraphs. Remember in school where we learned how to write a paragraph?

You have a main sentence, 2-3 sentences that support the main sentence, and finally a concluding sentence that ties together everything you said. The same thing is true with paragraphs. You have a thesis paragraph with your main point, then 3-5 supporting paragraphs, and a concluding paragraph.

You don't need much in order to get somebody to back, but it does have to make a compelling, clear, and concise case.

TIP #10: SEND UPDATES OFTEN

Throughout the campaign you need to update your backers at least once every 3 days. The average successful projects have given more than 10 updates. These can be raffle giveaways, or stretch goal announcements, or just a great day that you had. I like to offer weekly challenges on my campaigns, so every week I upload a new video for backers.

The point is that the backers need to be involved in your campaign throughout.

TIP #11: YOU DON'T HAVE TO DO A KICKSTARTER FOR YOUR DREAM PROJECT FIRST

If you've never raised money on Kickstarter before, then don't expect to raise several thousand dollars, especially if you have no network. You are much better served doing a project you can complete and fund, even if it's only $500 or less. Then you will have a baseline of your audience and be able to build from there.

Your goal is to get your feet wet and learn the ropes. It's not to stress yourself out chasing an impossible goal. You have an entire career to build up to your dream project.

TIP #12: PLEDGE TO OTHER KICKSTARTER PROJECTS

Kickstarter is a community, and people want to see that you are an active backer before you launch a project. Additionally, if you do back a lot of projects you can then email them during your campaign and ask them to introduce you to their audience. It might not work, but you are almost buying their time to consider your offer.

TIP #13: CONSIDER YOUR KICKSTARTER CATEGORY CAREFULLY

Some categories have a much more active community than others. Tech, design, and comics have very active communities. Publishing does not. You want to make sure you get a sense of the community

TIP #14: START YOUR KICKSTARTER ON A TUESDAY. END ON A THURSDAY

Studies show that Tuesday is the best day to begin a campaign. However, Wednesday and Thursday are very close to Tuesday. So much so to be within the study's margin of error. However, Thursday is far and away the best day to end a campaign. Thursday blew all other days of the week away by a statistically significant margin.

TIP #15: POST MORE TO SOCIAL MEDIA THAN YOU THINK NECESSARY BY A FACTOR OF 10

Only about 3% of people see your Facebook posts. Twitter has a shelf life of 15 minutes. So the people you think you are going to annoy probably haven't even seen your post. You need to post all the time in order to get the word out about your project.

Post when people back your campaign. Post when you've hit a milestone. Post everything, but make sure to keep changing your imagery so it doesn't get stale. It's the same reason McDonald's has 1,000 different billboards. The same image drowns in the background. People need new stimuli in order to keep engaged.

TIP #16: YOU NEED TO RAISE 30% OF YOUR KICKSTARTER FUNDING IN THE FIRST 48 HOURS

If you think you can raise $1,000, that means at least $300 needs to be raised in the first 48 in order to guarantee success. If you raise under 20% then your project will have a tough uphill battle. If you raise more than 50% it means your target was too low. 30% means you hit the nail on the head.

TIP #17: CONVEY THE WHY OF YOUR KICKSTARTER CAMPAIGN

Most campaigns are pretty good at describing what their product is. Some can even clearly discuss how they are going to bring it to market. Almost none convey why people should back their project or why they are uniquely qualified to bring the product to market.

The why is what makes people back, though. People are much more likely to back an unfinished product with a compelling why than a finished product that has none. The why is different for every product, but if there is no why, you will suffer much fewer backers and risk your campaign not funding.

TIP #18: BRING THE PASSION TO YOUR KICKSTARTER CAMPAIGN

If you can't show passion for your product, then nobody else will show passion either. You need to show extreme passion for your product to motivate others to get passionate about the product as well. Your passion is contagious, as is your lack of it. It needs to come through in your word, your social strategy, and definitely in your video.

TIP #19: MAKE SURE TO CALCULATE SHIPPING FOR YOUR KICKSTARTER CAREFULLY

Almost 10% of successfully funded products fail to deliver. The number one culprit in that failure is shipping. Sometimes rates go up, but sometimes it's because stretch goals change the weight and size of the box. Still other times it's because a product that was once media mail can no longer be shipped that way because certain incentives prevent it from being shipped in that way. Other times it can be because they didn't properly check shipping rates to all countries, and international shipping ate into all their costs.

You need to be very careful with shipping. It can add an undue burden on the unprepared creator. However, with some planning you can make sure it doesn't destroy your campaign and send you into debt fulfilling rewards.

TIP #20: KICKSTARTER TAKES 10% OFF THE TOP

Kickstarter takes 5% for their fees and 3-5% for all processing fees through their credit card vendor. Take this into account. Add 10% more buffer to your campaign to prevent failing to raise enough money.

If something is going wrong, or right, tell your backers. If you have something to say, say it. Don't hide anything. People are very forgiving if you are honest.

TIP #21: SCHEDULE POSTS BEFORE YOUR KICKSTARTER CAMPAIGN BEGINS

Buffer, Hootsuite, meet Edgar, Tweet Jukebox, and many others allow you to schedule a baseline of social media posts before your campaign begins. You will have other things to post as well, but you want to make sure you get the bulk of your updates out of the way early so that you aren't fretting about them when your campaign is live.

TIP #22: DOUBLE CHECK YOUR KICKSTARTER REWARDS

You can't change your rewards when your campaign is live. If you accidentally charge the wrong shipping price, or you need to change the tiers in any way once even one person backs, you can't. This often leads creators to create new tiers in order to fix what they screwed up. An ounce of preparation is priceless.

TIP #23: GIVE AN EARLY BIRD PERK TO YOUR FIRST-DAY KICKSTARTER BACKERS

The first 48 hours are critical to the success of the campaign, so reward those people who back early. It doesn't have to be much. Maybe the first-day backers get a free wallpaper, or maybe they get the digital rewards before anybody else. It doesn't have to be much, but that little gesture will help push people over the edge to back early.

TIP #24: MAKE YOUR KICKSTARTER CAMPAIGN A SPECTACLE

Kickstarter is the closest thing to an online comic-con that I've ever seen. You should be treating it as such by offering super cool, exclusive perks, doing live chats, engaging with your fans, and giving people something they can't get anywhere else. You could offer daily giveaways through raffles, or weekly videos.

You can do a Google hangout, or an AMA, but the simple fact is that Kickstarter is an event and the more you can treat it as such the more success you will have.

TIP #25: SET UP LAUNCH AND CLOSE EVENTS FOR YOUR CAMPAIGN

You can do this at your house, at a local comic book store, at a park, or a restaurant. The key is not to spend a bunch of money on the event, it's to get people excited about your project. If you are an artist, you can hold a show at a local gallery.

If you are a filmmaker, you can hold a trailer screening at a local theatre. You should hold these events the first and last day of your campaign to help drum up the more fervent enthusiasm possible during the most crucial times of your campaign.

TIP #26: BUILD PRESS RELATIONSHIPS EARLY

Emailing press contacts the day your campaign launches is too late. The press may have up to a six-month lead time on getting articles into their pipeline. However, if you aren't building your contacts well before then then the press won't even write a story about you.

You need to be fostering these contacts for months or years before you launch. Offer to do articles for them, meet them at cons, find them on social media, and treat them like humans just like you would for anybody else. The real question you need to ask is "how can I provide value in their lives?" When it's time to email about your project, then you need to make it easy for them to publish.

TIP #27: YOUR KICKSTARTER BACKERS WILL BE MOSTLY PEOPLE YOU KNOW

No matter how many emails you send to the press or how many cold contacts you make during your campaign, most people that back your project will be people you know for months or years before the campaign launches. That means you need the biggest network of energetic friends and fans before you ever hit the launch button. Remember, you can't be successful on crowdfunding without a crowd.

TIP #28: KICKSTARTER PLEDGE LEVELS SHOULD INCLUDE REWARDS FROM ALL PREVIOUS TIERS

You don't want people hesitating about backing a higher tier because they don't want to miss out on something they really wanted from a previous tier. You want it to be very easy for them to increase their pledge level.

Increasing existing pledges is a crucial part of the middle campaign lull, and any hesitation will prevent you from getting that extra pledge money.

TIP #29: MODEL PREVIOUS KICKSTARTER SUCCESS

Hundreds of other campaigns have done Kickstarter better than you in the past. They've succeeded and failed thousands of times. Use that to your advantage. Look through them all and find the points of commonality between them. Make sure to take note of the words they use, the imagery, and the reward levels that are consistent among the highest performers. Then, you can model that in your own campaign for the highest chance of success.

TIP #30: THE RIGHT TITLE IS CRITICAL FOR KICKSTARTER SUCCESS

With hundreds of projects to choose from, you only have a second to catch a backer's eye. With the way that

Kickstarter is set up, you basically get an image and a title to make a backer click on your link.

So you want to make sure your title is catchy AND that it uses all 60 characters to fully explain the reason somebody should click on your project. Almost all hyper-successful projects use a colon after the name of their project to state what the project is about. Make sure to utilize all 60 characters in order to give yourself the best chance for success.

And that's it. 30 tips to make sure your next Kickstarter goes off without a hitch.

THREE COUNTERINTUITIVE WAYS TO BOOST ENGAGEMENT DURING YOUR CROWDFUNDING CAMPAIGN

Most writers jump into crowdfunding with high hopes. We want to connect with our audience, rally a tribe of enthusiastic readers, and raise enough funds to bring our books to life. The standard approach is to make a polished pitch, share your campaign link, and hope your community grows. Yet despite good intentions, it can feel like your efforts fall flat. The marketplace is crowded, your inbox is quieter than you'd like, and those well-meaning "launch day" posts often slip by unnoticed.

What if the key to success is not about being more polished, but about embracing a few tactics that feel a bit odd at first glance? What if being raw, transparent, or even a bit vulnerable is what truly captures people's attention? Sometimes the best way to stand out is to go against the grain. In my experience, there are three unusual strategies that spark a different level of engagement. They might raise eyebrows at first, but they often lead to the strongest sense of community and the most enthusiastic backers.

Below, we will explore three ways to stir up meaningful connections in your crowdfunding campaign. They are not typical approaches, and that is precisely why they work.

1. SHOW YOUR WORK IN PROGRESS TO STRANGERS

It might feel risky to share unfinished stories, half-baked drafts, or raw ideas. Many writers want to wait until everything is perfect before letting anyone take a peek. In the world of crowdfunding, however, inviting strangers into your creative process can be one of the best ways to stand out. People love to see how the sausage is made. They appreciate being part of the journey and not just the finished product.

Most of us prefer to polish our manuscripts before anyone else sees them. We want our best foot forward at all times. Yet, when it comes to crowdfunding, there's something magical about giving people a peek behind the curtain. An unedited draft or a rough character sketch can make your audience feel like they're part of the journey instead of just spectators.

It also shows that you're human, and readers connect with vulnerability. When you say, "I'm still working out this plot hole, what do you think?" it invites real conversation. That kind of open dialogue helps build a sense of community around your project. By the time your campaign goes live, you won't be pitching to strangers. You'll be pitching to a group of people who feel like they're cheering on a friend.

How to do it: Pick small portions of your project that are interesting but not spoiler-heavy. You can share early sketches of a character design, the first few paragraphs of a draft, or a rough outline of your plot. Make it clear you are looking for honest reactions and feedback. This helps backers feel like they have a real stake in your creative process. The result is a powerful connection that goes well beyond a simple campaign link. By the time you launch, your followers will be cheering you on because they have already shared in your creative wins and challenges.

Why it feels counterintuitive: Many authors worry that early drafts will turn off readers who see flaws or underdeveloped ideas. In reality, most people relish that personal touch. They get to say, I remember when this was just a rough sketch. Now it is a finished piece on my shelf. Sharing behind-the-scenes updates also shows humility and invites your audience to root for your growth. This bond is exactly what helps your campaign gain momentum.

2. ASK FOR PARTICIPATION IN WAYS THAT ALTER THE STORY

Writers usually like to maintain full control. After all, it is your book. Why would you hand over any piece of it to your readers? The truth is that letting backers shape the work in small but meaningful ways can turn onlookers into superfans. If someone helps name a character or gets to pick an aspect of your worldbuilding, they will want to see how it all turns out.

This can feel like giving up control, but it can also create the most passionate fans you'll ever meet. Imagine if one of your reward tiers lets a backer name a side character or influence a small detail of the world you've created. That might sound terrifying if you're a perfectionist about every plot point. But backers who get to leave a personal stamp on your book will turn into lifelong supporters.

If letting someone pick a character name is too much, go smaller. Maybe they can choose a pet's name or suggest a minor detail that appears for just a scene or two. The important thing is that they see their idea in your final product. They'll tell friends and family, "I helped make that happen." That is genuine enthusiasm, and it lasts far beyond your campaign.

How to do it: Create a reward tier that allows contributors to influence a minor element of your story. You can offer a package where top-tier backers name a side character or decide a pet's breed or color. If you have a children's book, you could let someone rename the hero's best friend based on a loved one. The goal is to give backers a sense of ownership over a specific part of your story.

Why it feels counterintuitive: It can be nerve-racking to give away creative control. Yet in many cases, these personal touches make the story feel more alive. Readers who see their ideas woven into the book are more likely to rave about your work because they feel deeply connected to it. They are not just backing a campaign. They are contributing to the book's DNA.

3. NURTURE A SMALL, DEDICATED COMMUNITY INSTEAD OF A LARGE ONE

Most authors want the biggest crowd possible. Conventional wisdom says a larger audience means more support for your crowdfunding goal. A devoted community of 50 or 100 might bring you more success than an indifferent mass of thousands, though. Smaller groups foster genuine friendships among members. This leads to the kind of word-of-mouth support that can spark significant growth later.

Big audiences look impressive, but they can be surprisingly quiet. A small circle of 50 or 100 people who truly care about your project will often create more buzz than thousands of casual followers. When you have fewer people, you can get to know them as individuals. You can remember their names, see their questions, and respond in a personal way.

That sense of closeness turns casual fans into friends. They'll share your project with their circles because they've built a genuine relationship with you, not just seen a few promotional posts. These personal bonds lay the foundation for future campaigns. If you ever run another crowdfunding initiative, they'll be the first ones to come back, spread the word, and support you.

How to do it: Instead of worrying about hundreds of likes or follows on social media, focus on building a tight-knit space. This can be a dedicated subreddit, a private Discord server, or even a small Facebook group. Make sure everyone feels seen. Respond to comments quickly and ask for feedback on details that matter to them. If your community is small, it is easier to show up often and build those personal connections.

Why it feels counterintuitive: It is natural to want as many followers as possible. Yet when you are crowdfunding, genuine engagement is more powerful than the appearance of popularity. A close-knit group of fans is more likely to share your campaign and support future projects. It might seem like a small number now, but that loyal core can be your best asset when you are ready to launch.

Crowdfunding success is not about following the most polished strategies or chasing the largest audience. It's about fostering real engagement, building relationships, and making people feel like they are part of something special.

By inviting backers into the creative process, allowing them to contribute in small but meaningful ways, and focusing on a dedicated core of passionate supporters, a campaign becomes more than just a fundraising effort—it becomes a movement.

These tactics might seem unconventional at first, but they tap into something fundamental: people want to be seen, valued, and included. When a campaign goes beyond transactions and instead becomes a shared experience, it creates a level of enthusiasm and commitment that money alone can't buy.

The best campaigns are built on trust, collaboration, and the willingness to show up authentically. Those who embrace this mindset will not only run a successful campaign but also cultivate an engaged community ready to support future projects.

THE TWO MAJOR SUBSCRIPTION MODELS

There are basically two models you can use to build the continuity part of your author business.

We often call this "subscriptions," which is wholly accurate, but the reason I call it continuity is because we wouldn't say "I have a subscription to AAA." Instead, we generally call this a membership fee.

As such, a subscription is not broad enough to define the entirety of this category, even though it is basically the same action people take across all available options

In publishing, I see two types of continuity programs working well right now: *publication* and *association*.

In the *publication* model, customers pay to access the complete archive of a publisher's content. This includes any previously released work and any paid content created specifically for paid members.

You can find the publication model all over the internet, specifically in newspapers. Readers of *The Washington Post* or *The New York Times* are paying to access the reporting and additional content the newspaper provides.

That does not mean publications only provide articles for their readers. There are plenty of games on *The New York Times* site, and it's very possible to run this kind of model without publishing one word of text.

Take a website like World Anvil. With it, you can create detailed world maps for your universes. You pay a monthly fee, and in return, you receive access to the tool and the ability to use it. You might pay more for a commercial license, but your loyalty isn't really to the brand, it's to the product.

If you're reading this on Substack, you are likely familiar with the most popular outlet for the publication model among writers. Substack is the perfect venue for a publication model because the publication model relies on SEO and organic reach.

I don't necessarily believe in *Search* Engine Optimization, but I do believe in *Seek* Engine Optimization, which means when somebody actively is seeking for information, you need to make it easy for them to see you have what they need.

The more people who read the publication, the more who will become paid members to access a writer's archive. Therefore, it behooves the company to focus on virality and organic reach, because the publication itself is the reason people are paying.

There are two types of writers who thrive in the publication model.

A **reporter** is lean, fast, and relentlessly focused on whatever story is spiking public interest. They race from beat to beat, harvesting hard facts and fresh data to keep the publication's archive bristling with timely coverage.

By nailing the hot topic first and accurately, they funnel surges of search traffic into new subscribers who value speed and completeness more than personality.

A **columnist** is slow-burn, methodical, and intent on owning a topic through depth rather than velocity. Each opinion piece slots into an ever-expanding lattice of context and analysis that readers revisit for years, trusting the columnist's consistent worldview to decode events. The archive grows like a prairie, attracting subscribers who prize long-term insight and the steady accrual of expertise.

In general, if you are trying to "win" at the publication model, you probably don't want to paywall a ton of your content. Why? Because you're generally offering a single, lower-priced continuity price and are trying to scale through SEO and virality.

Substack is usually the best choice for the publication model because it has great discoverability, is optimized for SEO, and is good for organic reach.

If you're not taking advantage of the organic reach, then you are unlikely to benefit greatly from the publication model.

For those of you who don't resonate with this model, the second type of subscription that works well for authors is the ***association*** model, where you mainly pay to be part of a group of like-minded humans.

While you would be unlikely to identify yourself as a reader of *The Washington Post*, you are likely to identify yourself as a member of an association. This model is all about belonging.

When thinking about this model, you can connect it to organizations like Elks Lodge, the Boy/Girl Scouts, or even a bowling league. Yes, we join a bowling league because we like bowling, but we're mostly joining it for access to other like-minded people who have similar interests. If you think of the clubs you joined in high school, it is likely you got as much out of the friendships you made along the way then from the activities you did together.

Unlike publications that get by on virality, associations are all about offering perks to their members to help them connect together and form a deeper connection to the association. For this reason, people using an association model should paywall all or most of their content.

The association model is filled with goodwill and people who connect their identity to it. While you won't find a ton of free writers for *The Washington Post*, associations are largely built by volunteers.

Why? Because they feel the connection so deeply that they choose to volunteer their time to it. They are willing to devote a lot of time, energy, and effort to the organization because what they get out of it is a sense of belonging.

While Substack is perfect for a publication model, Patreon and Ream are great homes for an association model. Why? Well, Patreon comes from the word patron; that says it all.

A patron is somebody who feels a sense of belonging so deeply that they want to support the arts for no other reason than to support the arts. The best way to get somebody to develop a sense of belonging is to give them ways to deepen their connection to you.

In the publication model, readers don't need to form a deep connection to you. They form a deep connection to the topic and believe you are the ideal person to deliver the best information on that topic.

With an association model, people are really paying for a connection to you.

Patreon and Ream are better for the association model because they allow for multiple different tiers to love on your members and give lots of room for customization. Since people are partially connecting their identity with your association in this model, they are willing to spend quite a bit more to deepen that connection, which is something sorely lacking from Substack in specific and the publication model in general.

That doesn't mean people don't love publication models. It's just a different type of love.

I have been a subscriber to the *Washington Post* for years, but I don't consider it part of my identity. If they ever changed their model and stopped being the best place for me to get my news, I would stop subscribing and start paying somebody else.

One of the biggest problems I see in the author community is writers trying to start a publication model on Patreon or an association model on Substack. While Patreon has some cool ways to integrate with places like Wattpad, Webtoon, and Royal Road, their discoverability is terrible, especially if you produce NSFW content.

If you want to start a publication model business on Patreon, it would be best to plug into a website that has already chosen the publication model, like those I just mentioned.

Meanwhile, starting an association model on Substack prevents you from taking advantage of the multiple tiers and association benefits that make Patreon work so well for them.

This is not to say that you can't have success on Substack with an association model, or on Patreon with a publication model. Emma Gannon has a very successful Substack that is largely an association model. Meanwhile, N. K. Jemisin seems to be running a publication model on Patreon with lots of success.

It also doesn't mean you can't have both. I know many authors who have both a Substack and a Patreon simultaneously. Monica Leonelle calls this "going wide with your subscription business."

Like anything else with the Author Ecosystem, this is simply a lens through which to see your success.

So, which model are you using, publication or membership?

YOUR FIRST SALE PROBABLY WON'T (AND SHOULDN'T) BE YOUR MEMBERSHIP

Every writer wants to make gobs of money on their membership. They all want 100 or 1,000+ eager readers paying them monthly to read their beautiful words the day they launch their membership.

I've never met a writer who didn't want to wake up on the first of the month with a guaranteed $5k in their bank account. It's a lovely, wonderful dream.

Unfortunately, the *reality* is that subscriptions are the hardest game in town and getting harder with every passing month. People are *extremely* wary about committing to something long term even if it's cheaper than just buying it outright.

Companies aren't making it any easier by changing the rules to the game, deleting things from behind their paywall, and leaving people devastated that they don't have access to what they signed up for at the outset.

The unfortunate truth is that whether you're a new writer or just new to a reader, you're going to have a lot of trouble convincing somebody to give you money every month until they know, like, trust, and love your work.

Even then, it's very, very hard. I sell thousands of books and other products every year, but only 900 people are paying for my Substack membership out of 45,000+ subscribers.

That's a ton and I'm super grateful, but that money accounts for less than 5% of my overall revenue.

Yes, it's great that money exists and I'm very, very happy to have a base of support every year, but even after 2+ years spent building a membership, and writing the definitive book on the subject with Claire Venus called *How to Build a World Class Substack*, it is still incredibly hard to convince somebody to join my membership.

Meanwhile, 768 people backed the Kickstarter for our Substack book, and I've made over $100,000+ selling books this year, compared to just $17,000 in gross annualized revenue on Substack.

What I'm trying to say is that memberships are a tough first sale to a prospective reader, especially when they don't know your work.

What is a first sale? I know a lot of business terms are unintelligible jargon, but luckily this one means exactly how it sounds. *A first sale is the first thing your customer buys from you.*

Most writers have never thought about the customer journey from finding your work through falling in love with it, to buying and evangelizing for it. If you haven't thought about your customer journey, then get a sheet of paper, or a Miro board, and spend some time charting out how people find your publication, what you want them to do after they subscribe, and how they navigate your publication.

- Is it easy to fall in love with your work?
- Can they find your best work without confusion?
- Are they able to tell other people what to do without you chiming in?

If not, then it's time to do some work to make it easier for them, but let's focus on just that first sale for now, since it's probably the most important single step in this journey besides getting them into your ecosystem in the first place.

The most obvious flaw in most publications is that readers don't know what to do or how to buy from them.

This first sale needs to have a lot of intention behind it because making a customer part with their hard-earned money is a really hard and intimate task. While it's something we all do freely, it's not something anyone does lightly. ***Moving somebody from spending $0 to spending even $1 is harder than convincing somebody to go from spending $1 to spending $100.***

Before somebody pays for your work, they aren't convinced what you have to say has any value **to them**. Yes, your work has value for simply existing, but people only pay for things that have value to them.

So, the first thing we have to do is demonstrate the value our work has and who will get the most value from it. The clearer you are on who gets value from your work, the easier it is for somebody to decide whether they should pay for your work or not.

Once somebody finally agrees that your work has value *to their specific situation*, now it's about showing them how to support your work.

When designing this first sale, you can certainly keep piling value behind your paywall until people finally see and become paid members, but most writers don't have abundant resources at their disposal like I did when I started The Author Stack. Additionally, people are already wary about committing to a long-term subscription, even if it's just for a couple dollars.

Since turning on paid subscriptions, we have added close to 900 member-only interviews, courses, books, and more. Still, we are *only* converting 2% of our readers into paid members. Substack's metric say 5-10% is normal, but in my experience 2-3% is more normal, especially if you throw other products into the mix.

It turns out that if you have 45,000+ subscribers, 2% is a lot, but it's considerably less if you have 500 subscribers. So, how do we get more of those subscribers to buy from you?

If you don't have the kind of back catalog where you can stack a ton of value behind your paywall, then you might think about crafting a different kind of first sale, namely a one-off product like a book.

People are much more likely to buy your work if they can buy and consume a complete thought at once, even if it is considerably more expensive than a paid membership.

We're not even talking about creating something brand new. One of the best ways to get somebody to buy your work is to compile the best work from your blog into a

Direct Sales Strategy for Authors

book and either give it away (if you're trying to get subscribers) or sell it (if you're trying to make money).

Ideally, you would do both by compiling a **lead magnet** of 5,000-10,000 words to attract new subscribers with part of your work and additionally compiling a larger collection of 50,000-100,000 words into a book you sell.

This might seem like a ton of words, but every time I've asked somebody to go count how many words they've written, they're usually surprised they already have enough for a book.

Yes, you can also create a course, email series, podcast, or other product to sell, but if you're trying to attract people to read your work, then it's often best to make your first sale on something in the same format. Similarly, if you have a podcast, then compiling an audio course might be the best first sale for you.

For now, let's focus on making a book from your work.

Even if you have a fiction or memoir publication, you can compile a collection of short stories demonstrating how your ideal reader should feel reading your work. If you can get them to feel the same way in your lead magnet as they will feel reading your work, you'll go a long way to making people fall in love with your work.

I have an extensive guide on my publication on compiling a book into a blog that was ironically compiled into our Substack book, but it generally breaks down into four stages.

- **Stage 1: Gather everything into one place** - This is the simple but deliberate act of transferring all your work into a new document. It's really important that you do this by hand so you can see everything in one place and make some decisions about where to place things.

- **Stage 2: Bringing order to chaos** - Once you have everything in one place, it's time to bring order in the chaos. I recommend chunking everything into 3-5 different sections or themes. In this stage you'll be ruthlessly cutting everything that doesn't fit into a theme and curating those things that have the deepest resonance with your audience.
- **Stage 3: Filling in the gaps** - Once you've ruthlessly cut down to the bone, you'll likely find gaps you'll have to fill to make your book into a complete thought. I recommend writing these gaps onto your blog while you also use them in your book.
- **Stage 4: Tightening everything up** - Once you've got a good collection going, you should hire and editor and a proofreader, along with a cover designer, to make your work feel like a book.

I've done this so many times in my career and *it works* because people are desperate for curation. There are over 1,000 posts on my publication, and it's overwhelming. By focusing people on one specific topic, or product, I can fight that overwhelm and give them focus. *This is hugely valuable.*

People *want* to know where to look and how to consume your work in the correct order. Writers discount how important sequencing is to a reader, but the order by which you read something matters, and this kind of curation *always* has value and it's very easy for readers to see it.

I've been using this strategy for non-fiction since 2017, and what's great about it is that not only is it a low barrier of entry to new readers but it's also incredibly enticing for your ***existing readers*** who already pay you.

Nobody wants to dig back through your publication to find something that resonated with them, but they'll gladly buy a book that has the same information presented in the right order for easy reference.

Our Substack book was 100% compiled from Claire and my Substacks, with only small editorial embellishments, and it raised $18,348 from 768 backers. Before that, Monica Leonelle and I raised $30,372 from 715 backers for our *Direct Sales Mastery for Authors* books, which was 50% previously published material and 50% compiled from our publications. Back in 2023, I raised $5,282 from 278 backers for a weird collection called *This is NOT a Book*.

I even just did this with a short story collection called *Bulletins at the End of the World* that raised $3,972 from 153 backers.

We have a book live right now called *$8,333: 12 Concepts to Six Figures*, which has currently raised $9,417 from 453 backers that is 100% compiled from work in our previous books.

If you take the money we've raised through our books and added it to the money we've made straight from our membership, that's an additional $58,137 monetizing the same writing work a second time, more than 3x more than what we make just from our membership alone.

This has brought hundreds of new readers into our ecosystem while allowing us to monetize our work again and again and again. It's a lot easier to see what you'll get from our books than from exploring the morass of The Author Stack.

On top of that, ***new readers now have a very clear path to fall in love with our work.*** If you offer them a free, smaller compilation when they initially subscribe, it's even easier for them to find value *for them*. You're now guiding them on a journey through your best work and showing them why they should love your stuff.

You still might not have a ton of people who take you up on your paid subscription, but you've opened up a whole new line of business for people to support your work.

Every year, you could compile a collection of your work and launch it on Kickstarter (*my preferred launch platform*), your own blog, retailers, or anywhere to give people the chance to support you in more ways.

The more ways somebody has to support you, the more likely they will do so eventually.

HOW TO BUILD A SUSTAINABLE AND PROFITABLE SUBSCRIPTION INTO YOUR AUTHOR BUSINESS

I didn't start feeling comfortable in my business until I began seeing consistent, recurring revenue inside of it. For years, my sales were 100% launch-based. I would gobble up a ton of money in short bursts, and then watch it slowly wither back down to nothing before the next launch.

It was a nightmare because I could never plan for the future. Even when I was launching five times a year, I didn't feel safe investing in the future because every launch was still filled with uncertainty.

For years, I tried to set up some form of subscription income and always fell flat. I ran a Patreon in years past. I tried Ko-Fi and Buy Me a Coffee. I tested Kickstarter's short-lived Drip subscription platform. I even built an app to showcase my work. Nothing worked until I found Substack.

This is not a pitch for Substack or any specific platform. It's just a demonstration of how hard it is to set up a subscription that gains traction. Sure, some of it was the platform, but by the time I found that success I had significantly grown my audience for the better part of two years and had spent the last 15 years blogging and working with creators, not to mention growing my back catalog.

In my opinion, subscriptions are the hardest business model to get right, the hardest to get started, and the one with the highest upside if you can get the mechanics to work for you.

That said, I think most authors focus too hard on growing their subscription base in the short term instead of building it into their overall business model as a long-term engine for growth. Subscriptions will break your heart if you look at them as a short-term play instead of a long-term development. More than any other direct sales income stream, subscriptions should be measured across years instead of days, weeks, or months.

Internet marketing legend Russell Brunson calls subscriptions "'the lynchpin" of his business because it runs underneath and is critically important to everything else they do. For years, Brunson gave away a year of Clickfunnels to people who bought any of his other products. He used the immediate need for his course material to entice people to spend money in the short term and then used that material as a way to train people to use his product and build his recurring revenue in the long term.

Doing that allowed him to invest money back into marketing and grow his business to $30 million in annual revenue within a couple of years. Authors don't have $1,000 products in the same way Brunson does, but there's no reason they can't include either a free trial of their membership with every purchase of their product or offer it as a special add-on when somebody buys from their direct sales store.

Yes, this means whatever platform you use has to allow for couponing (unless you set up your subscription on your web store), but when I started my Substack I comped my entire email list a 90-day subscription that allowed them to see what I offered behind my paywall. I built my membership over 300 members in the first eight months using that strategy.

Another strategy I think could benefit authors is to run PBS-style pledge drives throughout the year. Even though you can donate to PBS throughout the year, they push hard during certain times of the year with telethons, special bonuses, and an intense focus on showing the value they provide.

Similarly, even though you should offer your paid membership throughout the year, consider designing a "pledge drive" when you first go paid (*with a sweet yearly discount for paid subscribers*) to build the critical mass necessary to devote time to your membership. Offer special pins, prints, or other bonuses for people who join during this special time, and try to get other creators with similar audiences to create a fun experience with you.

The hardest part of running a membership for paid subscribers is that whether there is one person or a thousand people behind a paywall, you have to do the work.

Once you have the initial drive complete, plan regular events to gather new members and convert free subscribers to paid ones. This has the added benefit of reminding your paid members why they subscribed in the first place to lower people dropping their subscriptions.

One of the biggest problems creators have with going paid is they feel like they have to always be on, but if you confine your ask to certain times of the year, then you can concentrate on the work of creating most of the year.

WHAT IS A SUBSCRIPTION?

A subscription is when somebody pays you consistently for something, in an author's case that something is usually book, or at least publishing, related. Publishing expert Michael Evans contends that authors have been running subscription businesses since the dawn of publishing. After all, our goal is to get readers to continue to read our work month after month, year after year. Now, we are just formalizing this process and taking control of the narrative in a way we never have been able to before by building our own membership.

A subscription gradually builds over time but requires a lot of time before it is successful.

Often subscription businesses talk about "hockey stick growth" which is the moment when their investment of time and resources starts to pay off and their membership income starts to look like a vertical line instead of a horizontal one. The problem is that nobody can tell you exactly when that moment will come. It might be in three months or three years. Meanwhile, you have to deliver every month even if you only have one subscriber.

Subscriptions allow you to build predictable money every month, test out products with dedicated fans, build an even deeper relationship with readers, and monetize your process earlier and with less refinement. That said, it's hard to get people to back your project unless they are superfans. You will likely have to offer enticement bonuses, free trials, or discounts to convince people to give your membership a try.

Usually, members of your subscription spend less money per month than they would during a book launch, but they spend it over a longer period. That said, "longer" does not mean forever, and one of the biggest problems with subscriptions is churn, or people canceling their membership.

We can endeavor to keep them happy by delivering consistent high-quality content and showing them the value of what we provide, but the average subscriber will spend somewhere between six months and three years in your membership before churning, depending on how good you are at retention.

There are hundreds of platforms to build your subscription business, but the most popular are Ream, Substack, Patreon, Ko-fi, and Buy Me a Coffee. You can also release chapter by chapter on Wattpad, Radish, Royal Road, and more, but you do not own the data.

Each of these platforms has negatives and positives associated with time I've talked about before, but I would recommend Ream for most fiction authors and Substack for most non-fiction authors.

You might even consider "going wide" with your membership and syndicating it across multiple platforms. Different people like different platforms, and it might make sense to gather subscribers on multiple and cross-post between them.

Most readers already have a favorite platform, and it might not even take that long to make this happen. You could think about having a main post on one platform and then have an assistant post on the other platforms and handle comments. Depending on the platform, you might be able to use Zapier or Pabbly to do this, too.

THREE LOW-STRESS MEMBERSHIP MODELS

While there are infinite ways to make a membership work for you, I wanted to highlight three models that work well for most authors just getting started.

In *the early release model*, you give your subscribers access to chapters before anyone else gets them. This is very easy if you are already writing and releasing books and you can release these pre-edited as well. You might think that nobody would pay for your pre-edited work, but how much would you pay for your favorite author's first drafts? This might seem like an egotistical question, but to your members, you are one of their favorite authors. They can't hang out with Stephen King or Nora Roberts, but they can hang out with you, which is pretty cool.

In *the additional content model*, you create brand-new material for your fans. This can be great for slow writers who have a dedicated fandom, or people who like deep world-building. Maybe you show off little vignettes you created to develop characters or lore baked into your books. Think of *The Silmarillion* or *The World of Ice and Fire*, and you get a sense of what kind of material you would create under this model.

In *the access model*, you give members special access to you. This could come in the form of secret chats with your subscribers, hosted live streams every month, or special events for them to enjoy. This is perfect for authors who are energized by being around their fans and have a larger-than-life personality. Readers love hanging out with authors and getting to pick their brains.

You'll likely do all of these but choose one of these to start and build from there depending on which feels right to you.

GETTING YOUR PUBLICATION READY FOR PRIME TIME

The number one thing that every writer can do to better improve their subscription is with better graphic design and making their page more aesthetically pleasing to visitors. So many subscriptions look bad to potential subscribers, especially in the cover imagery, and it immediately turns them off.

The reason I got traction in publishing was because I cared about my books looking as good as anything the Big 4 publishers put out. For some reason, authors understand how to make their books appealing to readers but have trouble translating those same skills to their subscriptions.

Most books that succeed have a base layer of quality to them where people can say "Yup, that's a book and it looks like it won't fall apart on me. The author looks like they can complete a story."

If you don't have that, people won't buy your book. Just because you have that doesn't mean they will buy it, of course, but if you don't have that they almost certainly won't give you a chance to earn their attention.

Even if they will buy either way, your job as a creator who wants to grow is to remove as many points where people can say no as possible. Any time somebody is given the choice to turn away, they likely will. We call this friction.

totally reasonable and much easier to swallow, along with being true.

ARE THEY NOT STOPPING, NOT CLICKING, OR NOT CONVERTING?

There are three big friction points you need to smooth out before you start getting traction for your subscription. Each of these points will make people turn away from your publication. Basically, you need to figure out if people are not stopping their scroll to check you out, if they are not clicking to read more once they stop, or if they are not converting into subscribers. We used to call this the three snaps because you're trying to wake people up and notice you.

If they aren't stopping, then you have a design problem. It means your imagery/text is not exciting enough to make the reader stop scrolling. This is the hardest part of the equation, honestly.

If they aren't clicking, it means you have a messaging problem. Perhaps you have a great image, but the headline isn't something your audience cares about, bores them, or something else in the messaging is preventing somebody from clicking.

If they aren't converting, then it means you are targeting the wrong people, or your text isn't crisp enough to get them excited. It could also be that you don't have enough places to join your email list throughout your article. Also, don't design every article for the same person, but the same kind of person. Everyone is going to find you at different places in their journey. You are technically the same person at every age, but you are very different, too. So, is your reader.

Once you fix those problems, you should be able to reliably get people into your subscription. It's not worth it to start scaling before you can fix these three problems. If you want to learn more about this, then read *Help! My Facebook Ads Suck*.

It helps to picture the design elements of a page that may be holding people back from diving into your publication.

Once you have a banger publication that looks great, then it's really about bringing people into your subscription environment. Before this point, your efforts likely won't bear much fruit. Now that you have the rest of your publication on fleek, you should start getting people you meet excited to join your community.

DEVELOPING A BRAND IDENTITY

How do we get readers past the friction points I defined above? The biggest part of it is about defining your **brand identity**.

Those words elicit groans from most authors I talk to, but a brand is nothing more than the promise you make to your readers that allows them to fall in love with your work.

Some authors have a very tight topic they write about, like Anne Rice. I know exactly what emotion I will get from her work every single time. Other authors, like David Sedaris, talk about a wide range of topics and I follow him for the unique way he looks at a wide range of topics.

Both of these authors have a great brand and a strong voice, but they go about defining their brands in very different ways.

I mean, can't you just close your eyes and picture David Sedaris's voice in your head? It's wry, and dry, and snarky, with a heavy dose of pathos that allows him to connect deeply with even the most mundane topics.

Now, do the same thing and picture Anne Rice. She hasn't spent nearly as much time on stage as David Sedaris, but can't you just picture a hauntingly beautiful love story between monstrous people played out over countless tragedies in an endless existence?

That voice you hear is their brand. It's the first step to defining your publication. Once you have that bit, it becomes easier to define the value proposition and unique selling point of your subscription.

Your ***value proposition*** is the tangible result somebody will get from subscribing to your membership. What is the special sauce somebody gets inside your community that will excite them to join?

Your ***unique selling point*** is simply what makes your product one of a kind. The unique selling point sets you apart from every other creative on the planet. It's something only you have. Your unique selling point might be that you print all your artwork in a certain way, or that you use certain materials. It might have to do with your worldview, the types of products you make, or the subject matter of your artwork. The unique selling point is something nobody else has except for you.

What's important to note here is that building your brand should not be about changing your writing to fit some predefined mold. It is about finding the language to define what you offer readers in a clear and concise manner.

A great exercise to help with this is to come up with a 7-word bio. Can you define your brand in seven words? Mine is *I help authors build better businesses.*

HOW TO THINK ABOUT METRICS

What about metrics? Should you be staring at your dashboard a hundred times a day? When are metrics good and when are they bad?

1. Metrics are good when they give you a baseline of what to expect in every post and can show you when you have a post that exceeds or underperforms those expectations.
2. Metrics are bad when you take those expectations, and they hamper you from doing something you want to do with your publication.

For instance, sometimes I'll have a post that performs way worse than others even though I'm sending them all to the same audience. When that happens, I'll change the headline and the imagery to see if that helps. Sometimes it does, but sometimes a post will only resonate with a small segment of your audience.

Tim Ferris says that he hopes that over the course of four podcast episodes, he can please 100% of his audience, but he only cares about servicing 25% of them with any given episode.

I think that's a really good metric to think about in your writing. *Will 25% of the people in your audience adore what you're writing?* Then, it's probably worth doing, even if you think it would be better to please them all. Hyper focusing your message to resonate deeply with a small subsection of people is how you cultivate superfans.

Making these decisions is a big part of finding your voice. If you only talk about things with mass appeal, then you'll likely start sounding like every other publication. When you focus on finding what makes your view unique, then that is when you can start separating yourself.

Weirdly, it's usually those niche articles that get the most paid members, which is the goal, right? *(Or one of the goals, at least,)* It's probably because people have never seen an article like it before, and if they think only you can deliver for them, they will see the value of joining.

Homogeneity is the death of small subscriptions. It's in embracing their unique voice that writers thrive and find an audience. Airbnb popularized the idea that the only way to scale is to do the unscalable, and sometimes that includes writing posts that absolutely can't find traction in the mass audience because they speak to very specific people who need to hear it.

Most of the metrics I've tracked over my career have made my business worse, not better. There are only three metrics that I care about these days.

- Net subscriber growth
- # of quality conversations per week
- $$$ in bank account

Some of my most beloved articles have almost no engagement. Most of my best-converting emails have no engagement. Most of my best subscribers are lurkers who just read religiously and never comment. I've not ever talked to many of the people who gave me the most money and most of our best evangelists are talking about my work without letting me know.

Maybe you care a lot about metrics, and that's fine, but for the most part, I think metrics are stupid.

That's not to say I don't care at all, but the three I mentioned are the only ones that have truly moved my business forward in any real way.

No matter what, if you track more than 3-5 metrics at any one time, it will be hard to have success moving any of them in a positive direction.

Subscriptions are hard. There's no way around that. The best subscriptions have been built over the course of years, not months. The best way to think about them is that they will grow over time as the best of your business grows.

In every case I can think of, creators spent a long time investing time and money into their membership before they started seeing significant growth. The frustrating part of a membership is that you have to treat it like you have 1,000 members even when you have 10.

The only consistent thing I have heard about memberships is that the creators were building, building, and building until one day it took off to the moon once their work caught on and they never looked back.

For this reason, authors should consider a low-risk, low-stress way to keep their membership going while they build it up without it costing them a ton of resources. I highlighted three different ways to build a low-stress membership depending on your personality.

I recommend starting with one of those options as your base. Then, once your membership catches on you can invest more and more of yourself into it, but if you give too much for too little return, then you'll likely burn out. I know it happened to me several times.

HOW TO BUILD AN EMAIL SEQUENCE FOR A BOOK LAUNCH

When I tell authors I send daily emails during a book launch, they look at me horrified. They tell me things like, *"I don't have anything to say,"* and, *"My readers will hate that."* I can only say, *"Yes, you do,"* and, *"No, they won't,"* so many times before it gets tedious. That amount of times is significantly fewer than the thousands of times I've had that conversation over the years. Today, I'm going to explain how you can send emails daily during a book launch without pissing off your audience, and give you the exact sequence I used along the way.

First things first. The number one thing I bet you're going to say after reading this is *"Well, sure, Russell, but that's for Kickstarter. It would never work with a real book launch"* which, like, rude.

A Kickstarter is just a fancy pre-order campaign for a book launch. Every single bit I use in my Kickstarter launches is cribbed right from more successful businesses, including authors.

Yes, if you launch into KU, a lot of this stuff is redundant because how much work do you have to do to get somebody to read a book for free except to show them that it exists?

If you're wide or direct with your books, though, you are asking people to part with money to purchase your book, and functionally it is the same as a Kickstarter. You are presenting a case for why you deserve their money.

Further, I would contend that KU no longer works for most authors and hasn't worked for many years for the majority of authors. If it works for you, great, but by all metrics I have seen, and colloquial data straight from the author's mouths, it works less well for almost everyone than it did in 2019.

Evidence? Most authors who called me ridiculous for focusing so heavily on direct sales have moved at least some of their books out of KU and are now building direct sales and wide business, which is much more work but comes with freedom and better access to fans. They wouldn't do that if it was working, but also they tell me it isn't working for them anymore.

So, if we can agree that a book by any other name reads as sweet, then hopefully we can agree that whether you sell a book on Amazon, Kobo, Kickstarter, or from your web store, you are working with similar buyer psychology. I will admit that if you are in KU, the mechanics are different, but even if you are working with a publisher, this is still critical information to absorb.

Second thing: Authors believe readers will tune out if you email them daily, even if for a short time. *This is bunk.* Assuming people signed up for your list ethically, then they are there to hear about your work.

Period.

Subscribers want to hear about your work. That's why they signed up for your email list.

Yes, some contingent prefers to hear from you rarely, which is why you should always give them a choice of how often to hear from you. At the end of my automation sequence for new readers, I ask them to tell me how often they want to hear from me; weekly, monthly, or just at launches. If they don't choose one, they agree to let me email them as often as I want, and I say that explicitly in the email.

If you do not choose any of the above, you will be sorted into my standard group, which usually receives weekly emails but during launches I do send more often.

Of course, I hope you'll stay signed up to get all my emails, as I really do try to give brand new information every single time I email you, even if it's multiple times a week, or even a day.

However, I very much want to give YOU the choice of how you hear from me, so you have a good experience.

I've sent 20,572 people through this sequence of which 792 chose to hear from me less frequently than "whenever I feel like it even if it's multiple times a day." *That's less than 4% of people.*

Not insignificant for sure, but 96% of people are perfectly cool hearing from me more often than weekly, as long as it's interesting. *The absolute worst thing you can be to a reader is boring, ever.*

Of course, that is a colloquial example, but there is a whole industry of daily emails like 1440 and Morning Brew with millions of people excited to hear from them every day.

The difference is they send new and interesting information with every email, and that's what we're going to help you fix about your launch sequence today. I'm going to show you how to send unique emails to your list they (should) love if they like your books.

I have raised $500,000+ on Kickstarter alone, and I use this strategy in almost every campaign.

Since I have 5+ launches a year it's a little harder, but if you're like most authors who launch 1-2 books a year, then there's no reason you shouldn't get some value out of this.

I'll be giving you my exact emails from multiple campaigns pulled together into what I think is an effective email sequence. These are only examples. Please don't flat out crib them. ***Use them as guidance and make your own.***

These emails are built upon the principle of buying triggers.

4 WEEKS FROM LAUNCH

When you're a month out from launch, you should already have your book on pre-order or your pre-launch Kickstarter page live. Therefore, ***your first email should be a simple announcement.*** You need your book on pre-order or your pre-launch page live so you can start collecting sales/interest.

Even if the book isn't 100% done, you should be able to use Book Brush or a similar service to generate a cover mockup, which is what I use to make mine. However, you can also just use the front cover to make your announcement.

THE END IS COMING...

Hi,

The end of The Obsidian Spindle Saga is coming in January.

Pre-launch link

This is my favorite series I've ever written. It contains several of my favorite books that I've ever written. If you have not read this series, and you love my work, then you will absolutely ADORE this series. If you have known of my work and been waiting to try something, then this is my best work.

Portal fantasy is my absolutely FAVORITE genre of fiction, whether it's The Wizard of Oz, Alice In Wonderland, The Magicians, His Dark Materials, The Lion, the Witch, and the Wardrobe, The Hazel Wood, Caraval, Ten Thousand Doors of January, Peter Pan, Neverwhere, or literally any other book about characters traveling to different places, worlds, realities, they are my jam. I poured all that love into this series.

Each book of The Obsidian Spindle Saga is told from multiple different perspectives from all across the world of Urgu, weaving together a narrative between them. This was the most complex project I've ever worked on, getting each character right, and telling different but cohesive stories between them.

One of the things I appreciate about Game of Thrones is that each character is not only rich and unique, but they also are having their own type of fantasy story. Sansa is having a story about political intrigue while John Snow is having a classic fantasy adventure story, all while Arya is having a coming-of-age fantasy story.

It's like 30-40 stories in one book.

These stories are quite pared down in comparison to Game of Thrones. Each book comes in around 275 pages compared to 500+, but I loved the idea that each story can be its own thing, and bring different elements of fantasy into it.

THREE WEEKS FROM LAUNCH

If you're using Kickstarter for the first time, then I recommend an email explaining what Kickstarter is and why you're using it. Otherwise, this can be substituted for a "why I love this series" or "history of this series" post.

[OPTION 1] WHAT IS KICKSTARTER?

Hey,

Even though this is my 17th campaign, it is always the first campaign for many people on my list, so I wanted to reach out and share with you how Kickstarter works in case you don't know.

KICKSTARTER LINK

How Does Pre-Ordering on Kickstarter Work

If you're new to Kickstarter, don't worry... it's a very easy, fun platform, one that's helped me bring tons of our awesome products to life over the years.

A few things to know if you choose to back:

1. *You can pledge today, and you will not be charged until the campaign is complete on **June 17th, 2021.***

2. *Kickstarter is an all-or-nothing funding platform, meaning we needed to raise our **$2,000 goal** (which we did in the first three hours) in order for the project to move forward. Your support means EVERYTHING, and we could not do this without you.*
3. *This campaign has a hard end of **Thursday, June 17th, 2021 at 8:00 PM**. You will need to pledge before then in order to secure your rewards for this campaign.*
4. *You can back today at any pledge level, and you have until the end of the campaign to up-or-downgrade your pledge.*
5. *The earlier you back, the more access you'll have to surprise campaign goodies and extras like our early bird perks, which go to backers ONLY. So, if you don't want to miss out on any of the fun, join us on Kickstarter today!*

Speaking of early bird perks, I put together an awesome bundle of EARLY BIRD perks.

Everybody who backs the campaign by Saturday night gets some amazing digital books, absolutely free, and included in your pledge.

All backers who pledge by Saturday (even for $1) get Lady Serra and the Draconian by Cat Banks, School for Dragons by Amy Wolf, Seeking the Salamander by Matt Harry and Stranger: Academy for Peculiars by Isadora Brown, absolutely free!

I am so super excited for this series. I spent the last three years building up the universe and writing these books. I can't wait to share it with you.

So, head over and check out the campaign right now to lock in these awesome rewards.

[OPTION 2] WHY WOULD YOU EVEN DO THIS TO A BELOVED CLASSIC, YOU MONSTER?

Hi,

Alice is my favorite literary character of all time. I love her so much that I have read both of her books at least 100 times. Every time I read it, I think it must have been written in a fever dream. The way Wonderland acts always makes me feel like she's on a strange, ethereal drug trip.

Then, I had this very weird idea that maybe it was a drug trip, and maybe the Red Queen had drugged everyone, which led me to the idea that maybe, just maybe, the people of Wonderland revolted against the Red Queen and the drugs were removed from the water supply.

Would that be a good thing for Wonderland? Certainly, it would seem that way, but what if the real world was too much to handle? What if reality kind of sucked? What would people do in order to get back to Wonderland? What would they give up? What would they risk?

Some would likely risk everything, and that led to building the whole world, full of characters you'll recognize, from Dormouse to Caterpillar to the White Queen, and locations you'll love like The Looking Glass Lounge.

*This is NOT a fantasy book. It's a straight thriller with nods to the original fairy tale. **I won't lie, this is VERY polarizing to Alice fans.** People who read the original story are split right down the middle on whether they love it or hate it.*

2 WEEKS BEFORE LAUNCH

Assuming you are launching a Kickstarter, the next email that should be sent is something previewing the actual page and asking your fans for feedback. This is a critical piece because your best fans will tell you what's wrong (or right) with your campaign. It also acts to get people excited about what they are going to get when your campaign goes live.

If you don't have a "page" then you can replace this with a "Read the first chapter" email, which you'll see later.

CAN YOU HELP ME?

Hi,

We're two weeks from the release of The Obsidian Spindle Saga and I need your help. You are always so helpful when I ask you to check out the build of the page and give me your input, so I'm asking you to do it again, if you have a minute.

Preview link

On top of giving me your thoughts, hopefully you'll get a better sense of the project, the world, and the characters. I love Kickstarter because it allows me to dive in deeper than a simple blurb and give you all the juicy details about the world.

While you're on the page, don't forget to click the top left to be notified when the books launch on June 1st.

Thanks so much!

ONE WEEK FROM LAUNCH

One week from launch is a great time to highlight a bonus people get for buying early. If you have direct access to your readers, it's easy to see who bought when, but you can also ask readers to submit their receipts to get their bonus.

Publishers do this all the time with new releases, and I think it's very smart. If you have a longer pre-order you can start this even earlier as a way to get people to buy the book before it launches.

EARLY BIRD PERKS ANNOUNCED...

Hey,

We're just one week out from the start of the Dragon Strife trilogy Kickstarter, and I'm just so so so excited. Maybe part of that is the insane amount of sugar I've had in the past week since being home, but I like to think it's because I love this story so much.

Notification link

Today, I am announcing some other books I love a whole lot, namely the early bird perks for this campaign.

*Everyone who backs in the first week of the campaign will receive digital copies of **Born of Magic** by Jack Holder, **Of Dreams and Dragons** by Karpov Kincade, **The Herebey Dragons** by Simon Birks, Eda Cagil Caglarirmak, and Lyndon White, and **Wildskies** book 1 by Melissa Hudson.*

I am so thrilled to include these books in this bundle, some of which are old friends and others are brand new that I just found in the past couple of months.

Whether you already love my work or haven't tried it yet, I think The Dragon Strife trilogy is the perfect series for you. Why? Let me tell you.

If you love my work, then you'll love this series because:

1. *It deals with a lot of the religious, political and socio economic themes of my previous work in a very interesting way while still being filled with action and pathos.*
2. *There are plenty of interesting characters and plot twists that will keep you turning the page.*
3. *It's a first person POV story from the perspective of a powerless woman who grows to become one of the most important people in the history of this world.*
4. *It is an empowering theme that will make you feel like you have agency in a world where there is mercilessly little of it.*
5. *Dragons!!!*

If you haven't tried my work before, then this is the perfect series for you because:

1. *It's a self-contained trilogy. There is a second trilogy that is planned, but there is no more of this particular story planned.*
2. *There is very little (if any) cursing.*
3. *Most of the violence happens off the page, so if you think my previous work is too gory, this series is for you.*
4. *There is a very serious and heavy romance theme through the books.*

5. *The character is a pacifist who abhors violence.*
6. *Most of the main conflict of these books are political and things don't get resolved with punchy punching like much of my most popular work. That's not to say there's no battles or violence, just that the plot hinges mostly on diplomacy and gathering allies together.*
7. *You won't have to remember a hundred different timelines and a thousand characters that hop around between books, or have a very long time commitment.*

I hope you'll join us next Tuesday to kick this year off right, and I hope you have a very happy and prosperous new year.

So those are the emails I would send before a launch. This cadence is only weekly, which should be doable for any author's audience. If you send less frequently than that, I highly recommend emailing earlier and giving people a chance to opt out of this launch or choose to remain at their current cadence.

I would send this email a few months early to give people a chance to take action. This can be as simple as adding something like this to your emails.

In a couple of months, I will be launching my next book and will be experimenting with a much more aggressive email strategy for two weeks. I think it will help you learn more about the world and history of this series, but if you'd like to opt out of it, please do x and I will make sure you are removed from those emails before they are sent.

As an author you should be able to test new things, and it might make sense to even say something about it being a test.

LAUNCH DAY

Regardless of your feelings about email, I don't think anyone will object to sending an email on launch day announcing your book is live.

THE OBSIDIAN SPINDLE SAGA KICKSTARTER IS LIVE!!!

Hey,

The Obsidian Spindle Saga is live on Kickstarter!!!

KICKSTARTER LINK

I am absolutely floored with how excited you all are for this book series, and I can't wait to share it with you!

Fairy tales are real.

Rose Briar is a diabetic, college student without insurance.

She's been scraping by through a combination of maxing out credit cards and relying upon the kindness of strangers.

Unfortunately, she's spent every dollar at her disposal. There's no money left to buy her life-saving insulin.

Without her medication, Rose falls into a diabetic coma. She tumbles into a deep slumber and wakes up in a fantastical place called the Dream Realm, where fairy tales and legends of old are still very much alive.

She has one chance to wake up.

She must trek across the world, visit the most powerful object in the land, the Obsidian Spindle, and entreat with the fates; the only beings powerful enough to send her soul back to Earth.

But evil forces don't want her to leave.

They will stop at nothing to capture her and make sure she never goes home again.

Now, with the help of her half-gorgon girlfriend and a mysterious red rider, Rose must race across the land fighting dragons, monsters, and the forces of the Wicked Witch, Nimue, in order to reach the Obsidian Spindle before her body dies on Earth and she's trapped in the Dream Realm forever.

Will she be able to wake up? Can she survive? That is the genesis of the Obsidian Spindle Saga (TOSS), and the first book The Sleeping Beauty.

For backing this series early, everybody who backs the campaign by Saturday night gets some amazing digital books, absolutely free, and included in your pledge.

All backers who pledge by Saturday (even for $1) get **Lady Serra and the Draconian** *by Cat Banks,* **School for Dragons** *by Amy Wolf,* **Seeking the Salamander** *by Matt Harry and* **Stranger: Academy for Peculiars** *by Isadora Brown, absolutely free!*

I am so super excited for this series. I spent the last three years building up the universe and writing these books. I can't wait to share it with you.

See you behind the backer wall.

DAY 2

I often send my "read the first chapter" email before the launch (as I talked about above), and only on books where it's not a spoiler. This is always one of my best-performing emails and yes, I add the whole first chapter right into the email.

READ THE FIRST CHAPTER OF THE DRAGON SCOURGE RIGHT IN YOUR BROWSER

Hey,

Happy New Year!

*The Kickstarter for **The Dragon Strife** trilogy is live on Kickstarter, and I wanted to share the first chapter with you so we can start the new year off right with some cool dragon books.*

Notification link

Today, I will die.

This wasn't a surprise to me. I had been preparing for it my whole life, but I never thought it would come until it crashed upon me this morning like a suffocating wave. Fifteen years on this Earth seemed like so much time, but now I realized how little of my life as a ceremonial sacrifice afforded me.

I was always an early bird. I woke with the sun, ready for the start of a new day. However, when the tender kiss of light touched my eyes on my final morning alive, I shut them tighter and pulled my sheets over my head. If I didn't face the day, then perhaps my death would never come.

I trained for this since I was a small child, but there is no amount of preparation that readied you for being swallowed by a dragon; its horrible, jagged teeth ripping through the white dress Sister Milka sewed special for the occasion and tearing your flesh as it gnashed against your virgin body.

Somebody softly knocked on the door to my room. "Gilda, we need to get started. Today is a big day."

Sacrifices were given every privilege. We wanted for nothing in our short lives, and after our deaths, those we loved were taken care of for the rest of their days. It was what the villagers bestowed upon us to assuage their guilt, and it was a small price to pay compared to the one we paid.

We were the salvation of the village, after all. It was only because of our noble sacrifice that the great dragon lord Ewig stayed satiated in his cave inside the volcano that loomed above us and didn't sweep down to destroy us.

That was the pact, cemented in blood a hundred years ago. Every five years, one of us must willingly walk to our deaths, and in return, the great dragon would watch over our village and prevent the great volcano that loomed over us from erupting, burying our village under its magma.

It was a great honor to be chosen as the sacrificial lamb. That was what the line they told me at least, but today it certainly didn't seem like an honor. It seemed like I was raised like a lamb for slaughter, provided every luxury to die at the right moment.

"Coming!" I said after a long pause. Sister Milka was a harsh and unforgiving mistress, and would not accept anything but perfection today, on my last day of life. Every day of my life she watched over me, training me to die well. Even now, at the end, she would not take her foot off my neck. Especially now, with so much on the line, with the prosperity of our town riding on the spillage of my blood before the clock struck midnight tonight.

I slipped my sandals on my feet and rose to stand. Before I answered the door, I spun and made my bed, as I was trained to do; the first sign of an uncluttered mind was a perfectly made bed. It was the least we could do to show how much we appreciated all we were given.

As I pulled the corner of the bed taut, I thought about not tucking in the final edge as a little sign of rebellion. However, when I tried to leave it mussed, pangs of guilt washed over me, until they were so overwhelming that, with shaking hands, I forced the last edge of my blanket in tightly.

Once I was dead, my house would become a museum, and my room a shrine, preserved exactly how I left it, and I didn't want my mother to have to explain that her perfect daughter died a slob. Why do I care what people think of me after my death?

With the bed made, I walked to the door and placed my hand on the knob. The minute I opened it, the machinations of my last hours, those that I trained for my whole life, would wash over me one after another.

"It's time to open this door, missy."

I closed my eyes and felt my breath against my chest, rising and lowering in slow, rhythmic time with the beating of my heart. They were small gestures, in the grand scheme, but right now, they were everything, and soon, much too soon, they would fall fallow and motionless forever.

What would happen after I took my final breath? According to the church, I would rise up into the sky and take my place among the stars, but what did they know?

The gods were long dead, and the dragons that remained had none of their love of humanity.

Banging came from the other side of the door, and Sister Milka's shrill voice cut through the air. "That's quite enough of this dawdling, Gilda! Open the door this instant."

Her shouting pulled me out of my calm, and I turned the doorknob. She exploded into the room, her trim frame and long face cutting an imposing image against the harsh light that fell into the room. She was not a big woman, but her presence filled my small room like none other.

"Good morning, mistress," I said, bowing my head to avoid her gaze. You never looked the nuns in the eyes.

She didn't answer for a long moment, busying herself with checking my room, inspecting my bed, and running her fingers across the top of my dresser, looking for dust. She rubbed her fingers together and gave a small nod. "I see your mother took this cleaning seriously."

I nodded to her, keeping my eyes turned to the ground. "Of course, mistress. She scrubbed all day and into the evening."

Sister Milka not only ran the monastery and school in town, but personally looked over all of us chosen for sacrifice, of which there were three at any time. It was a job she took seriously and had since taking her vows fifty years ago.

"Well, let me get a look at you," she said. "Stand up straight."

It was crucial that I not have a flaw or imperfection on my naked body, and for fifteen years I can't remember a time when I lifted a finger in manual labor. My mother made all my meals, or a member of the community would deliver it, and everything else was taken care of so I could keep myself flawless for my date with Ewig.

I dropped my nightgown to the floor and endured the intense gaze of Sister Milka as she examined every inch of me. Two years ago, I judged a livestock competition, and she looked at me like the other judges looked at the cattle on display, trying to decide which one would give the best meat.

"You need to shave every inch of you, except your hair," she said. "We do not want the great dragon lord to get a hairball now, do we?"

I shook my head. "No, mistress."

"Good, good." She placed her hands under my breasts and then pinched the sides of my waist. "You have put on decent weight in the past year, my dear. Yes, I think the dragon lord will be most impressed with you." Then she moved her

hand to my face and brushed her hand along my cheek. "You are truly one of my greatest girls. I am so proud of what you have become."

A compliment? She never gave me a compliment before. She had nothing but bitter, terse words for me, that stuck into my gut with pain and tore at my mind.

"T-thank you, mistress."

She moved her hand to my chin and pulled it up to meet her eyes, a great honor she afforded very few. "No, thank you, my dear. The sacrifice you make tonight is a greater burden than any child should bear."

Tears filled my eyes as I stared into Sister Milka's face. Her eyes were a cold, dark brown, and even though her words were kind, her face was sharp, and her voice terse, taking much of the tenderness from them.

"No need for that." Sister Milka pulled her hand from my face and slid a white handkerchief from her pocket. "This is a happy occasion, after all. Your sacrifice will save us all. There is no greater gift. Now, clean yourself up, and I will draw your bath."

That's just the beginning of the story. I hope you'll join us behind the backer wall, and you can read a few more chapters by clicking here.

Plus, if you back, you'll get a ton of awesome extra books.

*Everyone who backs in the first week of the campaign will receive digital copies of **Born of Magic** by Jack Holder, **Of Dreams and Dragons** by Karpov Kincade, **The Herebey Dragons** by Simon Birks, Eda Cagil Caglarirmak, and Lyndon White, and **Wildskies** book 1 by Melissa Hudson.*

And and and and and you can pick up the below 5" x 7" postcard print by backing @ the $22 or $75+ physical pledge levels.

Let's kick this year off right and fill it with magic and dragons.

DAY 3

On day three I like to talk about why I love this series and why I think they will love it, too. We've passed the nadir point of excitement, and so I try to bring it back to the heart of the book.

THE BEST SERIES I'VE EVER WRITTEN?

Hi,

I am prone to hyperbole and tend to downplay it when other people say that one book or another is the best book I've ever written.

*However, across the board everybody who has read The Obsidian Spindle Saga has said that it's not only **MY** best series, but it's one of their favorite series of all time…*

I've been developing this series since 2018, and I'm soooo excited to finally be able to talk about it. My small team of readers has been sworn to secrecy for YEARS and the cat is finally out of the bag, as they say.

The Obsidian Spindle Saga started with a simple premise. Knowing everything I knew about writing after finishing over a dozen novels, if I could go back and design my perfect series, the one that would stand the test of time and encapsulate everything I loved in the world, what would it be?

I gathered the pieces very quickly: a dash of fairy tales, a scoop of mythology, a spoonful of portal fantasy, a sprinkle of romance, a bit of social commentary, and a whole heap of worldbuilding, and when I sat back I realized…I wasn't a good enough writer to take on this series yet.

That doesn't mean my other books weren't good, but The Obsidian Spindle was more complicated than anything I had ever done.

I didn't know enough about writing romance, or YA, and I had never had a story written from multiple perspectives, so I set out on a very ambitious project, and wrote non-

stop for the next eighteen months, in order to learn everything I thought I needed to know in order to take on this series.

Some of those books you might have seen before. The Marked Ones, Invasion, The Void Calls Us Home all came from that process. Our Wannabe+ exclusive serial Anna and The Dark Place was the final book I wrote during that time span, the capstone that proved to me I was ready to write The Obsidian Spindle Saga.

This is the series I was talking about last year when I released all those books in my summer slate. All of those books were leading to this series.

And so, in June 2018 I wrote the first book in the series, The Sleeping Beauty, pouring everything I ever wanted to say into it, and spilling everything I loved onto the page.

I absolutely adored the book. I'm not the type of writer where things fall out of me easily. It's always a struggle to get a book on the page, and then I have to manhandle it to cooperate. I love all my book babies, but they are stubborn as a mule and twice as ornery most times.

That's not the case with this series. The Sleeping Beauty slid out quickly and without much struggle, almost exactly has I imagined it in my mind.

Then, over and over the people who read it said it was my best work ever, and even now, several dozen books later, they still mention The Sleeping Beauty, and the whole Obsidian Spindle Saga, as among their favorite series.

Here is the set-up for the whole book, and the whole universe.

Rose Briar is a diabetic, college student without insurance. She's been scraping by through a combination of maxing out credit cards and relying upon the kindness of strangers.

Unfortunately, she's spent every dollar at her disposal. There's no money left to buy her life-saving insulin.

Without her medication, Rose falls into a diabetic coma. She tumbles into a deep slumber and wakes up in a fantastical place called the Dream Realm, where fairy tales and legends of old are still very much alive.

She has one chance to wake up.

She must trek across the world, visit the most powerful object in the land, the Obsidian Spindle, and entreat with the fates; the only beings powerful enough to send her soul back to Earth.

But evil forces don't want her to leave. They will stop at nothing to capture her and make sure she never goes home again.

Now, with the help of her half-gorgon girlfriend and a mysterious red rider, Rose must race across the land fighting dragons, monsters, and the forces of the Wicked Witch, Nimue, in order to reach the Obsidian Spindle before her body dies on Earth and she's trapped in the Dream Realm forever.

Will she be able to wake up? Can she survive? That is the genesis of the Obsidian Spindle Saga, and the first book The Sleeping Beauty.

I invite you not to take my word for it, though. Try the first ten chapters for yourself by clicking here.

I hope you love it as much as me. I've currently written eight novels in this series, and the first four launch are live on Kickstarter now.

Kickstarter link

These first four books act as one complete thought and make up what I'm calling The Dream Realm arc of this series.

DAY 4

In most launches, I'll have an exclusive item people can only get during the initial launch period, and I want to highlight that during the first week of the campaign. I've probably hinted at it before, but I want to make sure to focus on it for one day.

THE SPECIAL POSTCARD PRINT

Hey,

We're still running through our first campaign of the year, but I wanted to talk for a second about the awesome 5" x 7" postcard print you can get for backing the campaign at either the $24 or $75+ physical book level.

Kickstarter link

My awesome cover designer, Paramita Bhattacharjee from The Complete Paramita has allowed me to print off a one-time reward of the virgin cover from The Dragon Scourge as a very special print.

I love it sooo much and we're NEVER going to reprint it. I'm only printing 100 of these and when they are gone, they are gone forever.

*Plus, everyone who backs in the first week of the campaign will receive digital copies of **Born of Magic** by Jack Holder, **Of Dreams and Dragons** by Karpov Kincade, **The Herebey Dragons** by Simon Birks, Eda Cagil Caglarirmak, and Lyndon White,*
*and **Wildskies** book 1 by Melissa Hudson.*

Gilda will die today. She has lived her whole life for one purpose—to be sacrificed to the great dragon lord, Ewig. And now, when the sun falls over the horizon, the time will come to fulfill her duty and walk to her death.

It was a fine life, but a lonely one. As payment for her service, the City Council lauded her with riches, allowed her to live in the lap of luxury, and fed her the finest food. She never knew hunger, or strife, even when others worked themselves to the bone and suffered starvation.

The others always resented her for that, but they never knew her pain. Theirs was a hard life, but at least they got to live it. Gilda never had that choice. She would not live to see adulthood. She would never be married or have children.

All that remained of her brief existence was to walk up the lonely volcano to the dragon's keep with honor, even though nobody treated her with any during her life.

Join her as she lives the last hours of her life, and find out what happens once she enters the dragon's cavern and everything changes; for her life, for her town, and for the world.

DAY 5

I usually launch on a Tuesday, and my early bird perks end on Sunday. Whether you have them for three days or ten days, make sure to make a big deal about them closing down. The urgency and FOMO associated with that will get some number of people off the fence.

LAST CHANCE FOR EARLY BIRD PERKS...

Hey,

*This is your last chance to lock in the early bird perks for the **Dragon Strife** trilogy.*

Kickstarter link

*Everyone who backs in the first week of the campaign will receive digital copies of **Born of Magic** by Jack Holder, **Of Dreams and Dragons** by Karpov Kincade, **The Herebey Dragons** by Simon Birks, Eda Cagil Caglarirmak, and Lyndon White, and **Wildskies** book 1 by Melissa Hudson.*

Gilda will die today. She has lived her whole life for one purpose—to be sacrificed to the great dragon lord, Ewig. And now, when the sun falls over the horizon, the time will come to fulfill her duty and walk to her death.

It was a fine life, but a lonely one. As payment for her service, the City Council lauded her with riches, allowed her to live in the lap of luxury, and fed her the finest food. She never knew hunger, or strife, even when others worked themselves to the bone and suffered starvation.

The others always resented her for that, but they never knew her pain. Theirs was a hard life, but at least they got to live it. Gilda never had that choice. She would not live to see adulthood. She would never be married or have children.

All that remained of her brief existence was to walk up the lonely volcano to the dragon's keep with honor, even though nobody treated her with any during her life.

Join her as she lives the last hours of her life, and find out what happens once she enters the dragon's cavern and everything changes; for her life, for her town, and for the world.

Plus, you can get an awesome 5" x 7" postcard print for backing the campaign at either the $22 or $75+ physical book level.

Hope to see you behind the backer wall to start the new year.

END WEEK 1

Now, we've finished the first week. Hopefully, you can see that every email sent so far highlights a different aspect of the launch and gives readers a different angle to get excited about in a way that even people who already bought would be happy to get them, too.

For week 2, I'm focused on what's called the sideways sales letter, a classic marketing technique that works like gangbusters.

The goal here is to break apart all the knowledge a reader needs to get excited to read the series and spoon-feed it to them over several days.

This is because nobody ever reads every part of a page, and most people discount things they don't understand. If you build a narrative, then you'll have a better chance of getting people to pay attention.

WEEK 2

DAY 8

I already shared a post about "the best series I've ever written," which kind of does the part about why you love the series, but I think you need to share how much you love your work multiple times throughout your launch in different ways. If you've already launched books in this series, you could also send a collection of testimonials about your other books. Social proof is very important to get people off the fence.

[OPTION 1] WHY DO I LOVE THE DRAGON STRIFE TRILOGY?

Hey,

*The Kickstarter for **The Dragon Strife** trilogy is in its second week and I wanna tell you more about why I love it so so much.*

Kickstarter link

So, why do I love this story?

Because I'm obsessed with writing stories where people with no power end up changing the world, and Dragon Strife may be the best encapsulation of that in all my books.

Gilda is literally a sacrifice. Her entire town, including her mother, have agreed to allow her to die in the most brutal way possible; by being eaten alive by a dragon.

Nobody cares about her, except for the other people who have been forced to die, and yet...

...those same people become the key to saving everything.

It's the overriding thesis to all my works; those people who you look over and pass by are just as important as anyone else, and if you raise them up, they might just change the world.

Gilda starts as a sacrifice, but she becomes so much more, and it's empowering as fuck to read. People have always told me the thing they like about my work is that people have agency in a world where they feel like they have none.

I love that about my work, and I definitely lean into it hardcore with this book. I can't wait to share it with you.

Plus, if you back, you'll get a ton of awesome extra books. Usually, I throw the most perks to early bird backers, but this campaign I'm trying something different, and unlocking a huge slew of new perks for people who back by the end of the campaign.

Everyone who backs by the end of this week will receive digital copies of **Mythic Creature Trainer #1** *by Rene Pfitzer,* **Luminous Ages #1**

by Antonios Christou, **Dragonwar** *by Mirren Hogan,* **School of Dragons**

by Amy Wolf, **Gods of Aazurn** *by Gary Scott Beatty and* **Gage and the Dragon's Tear #1** *by Patrick Kellner,*

Donny Hadiwidjaja, Bryan Valenza, Ed Dukeshire, Marta Tanrikulu, and Randy Michaels.

And and and and and you can pick up the below 5" x 7" postcard print by backing @ the $22 or $75+ physical pledge levels.

I hope you'll join us behind the backer wall to kick this year off right, filled with magic and dragons.

[OPTION 2] THE REVIEWS ARE IN...

Hey,

We crested over $6,000 last night, which is amazing. I'm absolutely blown away by how much love you all have shown The Godsverse Chronicles.

KICKSTARTER LINK

Today I didn't want you to hear from me. I wanted to show you some of the reviews from the Godsverse throughout the years. One of the awesome parts of adding to a series that's already out is that people have read it already!

These are readers, just like you, who have read and reviewed the books on Goodreads and Amazon.

This campaign features THREE NEW never before seen novels, including:

- *And Conquest Followed Behind Them, an Avengers-style team-up book between Katrina, Kimberly, Akta, and Julia as they fight to prevent Ragnarok.*
- *And Chaos Followed Behind Them, an Avengers-style team book between Katrina, Kimberly, Akta, Julia, and Rebecca where the women of the Godsverse fight to stop the end of the universe.*

- *And Darkness Followed Behind Her, three story collection starring fan-favorite Kimberly before, during, and after the events of And Conquest Followed Behind Them, including a story set during the first days of the Apocalypse.*

The Godverse takes my two most popular graphic novels, Katrina Hates the Dead/Katrina Hates Dead Shit and Pixie Dust, novelizes them, and adds FIFTEEN additional stories set across 13,000 years!

These books are exciting, action-adventure mythological fantasy novels steeped in mythology, then filled with humor, action, and fun.

If you've travelled through the Godsverse before, these new adventures will fill in gaps in the universe you have asked me about for years, and if you're new to the Godsverse, there has never been a better time to get started.

*Plus, everyone who backs by Saturday will get digital copies of **The Twelve Labors of Nick** by Amy Wolf, **A Tribe of Kassia** by Tom Leveen, **Harsh Line** by Ann Gimpel, and **Snowed** by Maria Alexander!*

So, head over and check out the campaign right now to lock in these awesome rewards.

DAY 9

For this series specifically, I was using the heroine's journey, which operates much differently than the hero's journey, and I wanted to highlight that for people who might not have wanted to read another typical adventure series. If you have anything like that, this is a perfect time to write that email. If you don't have that, consider taking an unfair objection you hear about your series or genre and talking about how your book is different.

[OPTION 1] THE HEROINE'S JOURNEY...

Hey,

*The Kickstarter for **The Dragon Strife** trilogy is in its second week and I wanna tell you more about why I love it so so much.*

Kickstarter link

So, most of us know the hero's journey, where a person goes out into the world and finds their destiny.

What we don't talk about enough is the heroine's journey, which is a thing, and one of the driving forces in a lot of my work.

In the heroine's journey, the main character doesn't go out and get imbued with power from their journey. Instead, they learn to use the power that was inside themselves the whole time.

It's one of the things I love most about Captain Marvel. She does not find power, she learns to use the power that was inside of her the whole time.

The Dragon Strife trilogy is very much about Gilda finding a power that was inside herself the whole time; a power that not only didn't she know was there, but that people told her didn't exist.

Yes, there are many elements of the hero's journey in the story, but at the end it's a trilogy about Gilda's inward journey from sacrifice to hero by using the unique things about her that people always told her weren't important.

People have always told me that my stories made them feel empowered, like they had agency in a world that tried to convince them they didn't.

I believe the true journey of our lives isn't going out and finding glory, but learning to live with the unique, wonderful humans that we are, and that using what makes us unique is what makes us a hero.

The Dragon Strife trilogy is very much about that, and I hope it's something you latch on to, and something that you can share with everyone in your life that had felt powerless or weak because they don't see the wonderful person they are, and how that makes them uniquely special.

I hope you'll join us on this journey.

Plus, if you back, you'll get a ton of awesome extra books. Usually, I throw the most perks to early bird backers, but this campaign I'm trying something different, and unlocking a huge slew of new perks for people who back by the end of the campaign.

*Everyone who backs by the end of this week will receive digital copies of **Mythic Creature Trainer #1** by Rene Pfitzer, **Luminous Ages #1***

 *by Antonios Christou, **Dragonwar** by Mirren Hogan, **School of Dragons***

 *by Amy Wolf, **Gods of Aazurn** by Gary Scott Beatty and **Gage and the Dragon's Tear #1** by Patrick Kellner, Donny Hadiwidjaja, Bryan Valenza, Ed Dukeshire, Marta Tanrikulu, and Randy Michaels.*

And and and and and you can pick up the below 5" x 7" postcard print by backing @ the $22 or $75+ physical pledge levels.

I hope you'll join us behind the backer wall to kick this year off right, filled with magic and dragons.

[OPTION 2] "WHY WOULD I READ ANYTHING BUT ROMANCE?"

Hi,

Some years ago I was at a conference talking to attendees, as I often do, and I got into a conversation with a woman.

I asked her what she read, to which she said romance, and then told her I wrote fantasy. I asked her if she read anything but romance, and she said something along the order of:

"Why would I read anything but romance? It's the only genre where women are treated well and can expect to have a happy ending."

I went to respond, but the words didn't come out, because she's kind of right. Romance is the one genre where women can reasonably be expected to have rich inner lives and have their needs centered in a narrative.

In pretty much any other genre, they are generally used as side characters, emotional baggage, and "fridged" to give the protagonist a reason to go on their quest.

This is a gross generalization, but it made complete sense to me. I went back to my own work with this lens, and it made me realize why a lot of women probably really like my work...

...because like romance, the women of the Godsverse lead both rich inner and outer lives. They have agency in the story and can actively work for a happy ending.

Are their lives perfect? No. Do they struggle? All the time. Am I sometimes sadistic with what they have to go through? Yes.

But the women are all fully developed with their own inner and outer lives. People don't talk down to them (and those that do eventually get their teeth knocked out), and they aren't placed into the narrative just so the main character has a reason to go on their quest.

There is little romance in The Godsverse Chronicles, but I've thought of that woman often when I write books, and it gave me a guiding direction in my writing.

If that is why you mostly read romance, or you're looking for a series where the main characters have agency and lead rich lives, then I hope you'll try The Godsverse Chronicles.

As I mentioned before, I write noblebright fantasy, which means that the good guys are trying to improve the universe, and even though they face struggles, they do the right thing when the pressure is on them.

Plus, they're pretty funny, and really fun books, even though there's often dark themes that run through them.

Are you ready to dive into The Godsverse, whether for the 1st, 8th, or 11th time? Then, make sure to check out our Kickstarter.

Kickstarter link

Plus, backers this week get some really cool early bird perks. Everyone who backs by 5/29 (including people *who've already backed), get digital copies of **The Mantle** by WT Meadows and Chrishaun Keller-Hanna, **A Curse, A Key, & a Corkscrew** by Anna McCluskey, **Merlin's Secret** by Jamie Davis, and **The Shadow Reader** by Sandy Williams.*

Hope to see you behind the backer wall.

DAY 10

On this day, it's good to talk about the world your book is set in (even if it's the real world talk about why you chose that city/time/setting).

THE WORLD OF DRAGON STRIFE

Hey,

It's been a week since I launched the Obsidian Spindle Saga, and I'm so so so so so excited for how far we've come, and how supportive you are of my...well it would not be untrue to call it my obsession over the past three years.

KICKSTARTER LINK

So, what is the Obsidian Spindle?

The Obsidian Spindle is one of the most powerful objects in the universe. There is one in every dimension and every inhabited planet in the known galaxy. It is a transport hub between planets for gods and magical creatures, but it is also a focus for magical energy, as it takes an incredible amount of power to make it work.

Think of it like The Wheel of Time, or the Dark Tower. It is a powerful magical object that much of the story relies on and many of the character's destinies depend.

In the Dream Realm, the Fates live inside the locked tower of the Obsidian Spindle, and Rose must find a way to open it if she ever hopes to return back to Earth before her body dies and she's stuck in the Dream Realm forever.

Every "arc" of this series will feature different realms and characters. These first four books are what I am calling The Dream Realm arc.

Each book tells a good chunk of the story with a satisfying conclusion, but there are cliffhangers between books that are only resolved at the end of each arc, and each arc also has a beginning, middle, and end.

This week, you get SIX digital books for backing the Obsidian Spindle Saga (including if you already backed).

*All backers who pledge by Saturday (even for $1) get **Secret of Moldara** by Brianne Earhart, **The Farshore Chronicles** box set (that's THREE books) by Justin Fike, **Sanyare** by Megan Haskell, and **Crimson Fire** by Mirren Hogan!*

DAY 11

Aside from the world, the characters are the other biggest reasons a person buys a book. Depending on the genre, people might buy for a character or a world more, so we should talk today about the main characters.

WHO ARE THE MAIN CHARACTERS?

Hey,

There's only one week left to back the Obsidian Spindle Saga, and we haven't even talked about any of the characters yet.

KICKSTARTER LINK

So, who are the main characters of The Obsidian Spindle Saga (TOSS)?

Each book of The Obsidian Spindle Saga is told from multiple different perspectives from all across the world of Urgu, weaving together a narrative between them.

This was the most complex project I've ever worked on, getting each character right, and telling different but cohesive stories between them.

One of the things I appreciate about Game of Thrones is that each character is not only rich and unique, but they also are having their own type of fantasy story. Sansa is having a story about political intrigue while John Snow is having a classic fantasy adventure story, all while Arya is having a coming-of-age fantasy story.

It's like 30-40 stories in one book.

These stories are quite pared down in comparison to Game of Thrones. Each book comes in around 275 pages compared to 500+, but I loved the idea that each story can be its own thing, and bring different elements of fantasy into it.

Rose *- The narrative of The Obsidian Spindle Saga rotates quite heavily around Rose. She plays the role of the Sleeping Beauty in our narrative, but also Alice, and Dorothy, as she is the character we see the first moments of the Dream Realm through, and the one filled with the most wonder about what she's seeing. Rose is a college student with no magical powers, who is so poor she lives in a van in the school parking lot with her half-gorgon girlfriend, Chelle. She is also a diabetic, who often has to* *choose between medication and eating, which is what sets her on her path.*

Chelle - *Chelle is Rose's half-gorgon girlfriend. As a "monster," she has been chased and hunted for her whole life by monster hunters trying to make a name for themselves. Her mother was slaughtered and her parts sold on the black market. She has some of her mother's gorgon powers, and also other magical powers. She has learned to defend herself and protect the ones she loves.*

Nimue - *The Wicked Witch of our universe is the ruler of the Land of Oz. She deposed the previous ruler, Ozma, and has ruled for the last hundred years, since the time Hypnos vanished without a trace. She is the most powerful witch in Urgu, as she was blessed by Hera, and is working in consort with her to open the locked door to the Obsidian Spindle and return to Earth by any means necessary.*

Red - *Red is the titular Red Riding Hood in our universe. She is one of Ozma's royal guards and has searched for a way to depose the Wicked Witch and return Hypnos to the world for the last century. She believes that Rose is the key to bringing back Hypnos and restoring order in Urgu, and will do anything to protect her.*

Queen Aine - *The ruler of the Forbidden Forest, Queen Aine is a powerful Unseelie fairy that led a brutal war, wiping out the Seelie and consolidating power. She is ruthless about obtaining and maintaining power. However, she is very adept at diplomacy, and molding wills to her own ends.*

Each book in this arc follows these characters along their journey. As you can see above, there are many different paths these characters will walk over the course of this first arc, as they try to keep and maintain power, while attempting to mold fate to their will.

This week, you get SIX digital books for backing the Obsidian Spindle Saga (including if you already backed).

*All backers who pledge by Saturday (even for $1) get **Secret of Moldara** by Brianne Earhart, **The Farshore Chronicles** box set (that's THREE books) by Justin Fike, **Sanyare** by Megan Haskell, and **Crimson Fire** by Mirren Hogan!*

DAY 12

We've talked about objections to your work, but I also love including things I've heard about my work and how it makes them feel. This is a bit different from reviews, but it hits the same feelings of "Other people have read these books and like them so maybe I should, too".

"YOUR BOOKS MAKE ME FEEL LIKE I HAVE AGENCY IN A CHAOTIC WORLD..."

Hi,

There was a book released last year called "7 Figure Fiction" which talked about the "universal fantasy" your books offered readers.

It set the author world on fire as writers asked themselves what special thing do they offer readers with their books.

I did not get worked up into a tizzy about it, because for years readers have told me exactly what my books gave them; agency.

Throughout my career, readers have consistently told me that my books "made them feel like they had agency in a world where they often felt like they had none."

This is especially true in The Godsverse Chronicles, which is about strong-willed women who fight against the fates the gods have given them. They take their destiny into their own hands to influence the direction of the universe on a cosmic level.

These women are rarely endowed with powers, or godhood. They are usually just ordinary women, or fairies, who are sick of their plight and have had too much foisted onto their shoulders.

Who hasn't felt that in the past two years especially?

I know I have, and I also know that writing these books made me feel powerful; they made me feel like I had some control over my destiny, just like the women I wrote about.

Yes, they face trials, but they never give up.

I write what is generally referred to as noblebright fantasy, which is the opposite of grimdark. It's about good, or nebulously good, characters who do the right thing for the right reasons.

These women are not Pollyannas, and sometimes they're not even very good at being good, but they strive to make the world a better place.

The world could use more of that, frankly, and I'm very proud to bring that energy into my worlds, and hopefully, into yours.

Because who doesn't want to feel like they have agency in a world that often seems intent to take it away from you.

What do you think? Have you read the Godsverse Chronicles? Is that how the books made you feel?

Are you ready to dive into The Godsverse, whether for the 1st, 8th, or 11th time? Then, make sure to check out our Kickstarter.

Kickstarter link

*Plus, backers this week get some really cool early bird perks. Everyone who backs by 5/29 (including people who've already backed), get digital copies of **The Mantle** by WT Meadows and Chrishaun Keller-Hanna, **A Curse, A Key, & a Corkscrew** by Anna McCluskey, **Merlin's Secret** by Jamie Davis, and **The Shadow Reader** by Sandy Williams.*

Hope to see you behind the backer wall.

DAY 13

We're nearing the end, so now we switch to talking about how there's only one day left either of the launch, or the special offer, or whatever you're doing.

ONE DAY LEFT...

Hey,

There's just one day left to back the Dragon Strife trilogy on Kickstarter and get all the amazing perks we unlocked this week.

Kickstarter link

Usually, I throw the most perks to early bird backers, but this campaign I'm trying something different and unlocking a huge slew of new perks for people who back by the end of the campaign on Saturday.

I am so excited for these books.

*Everyone who backs in the first week of the campaign will receive digital copies of **Mythic Creature Trainer #1** by Rene Pfitzer, **Luminous Ages #1** by Antonios Christou, **Dragonwar** by Mirren Hogan, **School of Dragons** by Amy Wolf, **Gods of Aazurn** by Gary Scott Beatty and **Gage and the Dragon's Tear #1** by Patrick Kellner, Donny Hadiwidjaja, Bryan Valenza, Ed Dukeshire, Marta Tanrikulu, and Randy Michaels.*

And and and and and you can pick up the below 5" x 7" postcard print by backing @ the $22 or $75+ physical pledge levels. I hope you'll join us behind the backer wall to kick this year off right, filled with magic and dragons.

I hope you'll join us behind the backer wall to kick this year off right, filled with magic and dragons.

DAY 14

This is it, the last day. You'd be surprised how many people wait until the last minute to make a decision, so you should absolutely send an email on the last day to give people one last nudge.

JUST HOURS LEFT...

Hey,

There are only a few hours left to back the Dragon Strife trilogy on Kickstarter and get all the amazing perks we unlocked this week.

Kickstarter link

Usually, I throw the most perks to early bird backers, but this campaign I'm trying something different and unlocking a huge slew of new perks for people who back by the end of the campaign on Saturday.

I am so excited for these books.

*Everyone who backs in the first week of the campaign will receive digital copies of **Mythic Creature Trainer** #1 by Rene Pfitzer, **Luminous Ages** #1 by Antonios Christou, **Dragonwar** by Mirren Hogan, **School of Dragons** by Amy Wolf, **Gods of Aazurn** by Gary Scott Beatty and **Gage and the Dragon's Tear** #1 by Patrick Kellner, Donny Hadiwidjaja, Bryan Valenza, Ed Dukeshire, Marta Tanrikulu, and Randy Michaels.*

And and and and and you can pick up the below 5" x 7" postcard print by backing @ the $22 or $75+ physical pledge levels. I hope you'll join us behind the backer wall to kick this year off right, filled with magic and dragons.

This is only one example, but I hope you have an idea about how you can send more emails without burning out your audience. Even if you only send a couple emails about your launch, please try to vary them up and keep them interesting.

The cardinal sin of email is being boring.

Sending the same email is boring. Nobody wants to be spammed with the same information, but if you can remain interesting people will eat that up all day. You can send more emails than you think and you're more interesting than you believe.

The natural fear to have in all of this is that everyone will unsubscribe. So, I will tell you a story. A few days before writing this, I sent an offer to 5,000 leads I've gotten through Sparkloop. It was a bloodbath with 2% of people unsubscribing. To give you some context, .5% is the top threshold for most providers, so this was 4x higher than that.

I would consider that a slaughter, and yet, still 98% of people did not unsubscribe and it still had a 46% open rate. Even if that carried on for all 14 days of this sequence, I would still only lose 1,400 subscribers, far from everyone unsubscribing.

Think about it. I basically email people every day, but as far as I know, the majority haven't unsubscribed. I would guess it's because either:

- They like me so they put up with my nonsense
- They know it's coming from a good place
- They are entertained by it or
- They gain something from every email enough to put up with the nonsense of sending so much.

No, you can't email every day, *unless you are entertaining about it and send new information.* Then, you can do just about whatever you want.

Assuming you are using a program like Convertkit, you can also add a bit to your emails that says, "If you want to stay on my list, but you don't want to hear about this launch, click here" and then make something like "NO X LAUNCH" tag, and then make sure to exclude those people, and then they won't get those emails.

Here's the thing: Bookbub sends me daily emails, so does Chirp, and so do many, many people, but I enjoy getting them, so it's okay. Once you start believing that YOU are somebody's favorite email, the rest kind of falls into place.

If somebody doesn't feel that way, then I don't want them there anyway.

HOW TO PRINT BOOKS FOR FUN AND PROFIT

I've always been fascinated with printing books. Even before I started printing them myself, back before I even considered myself a writer, I loved the feel and smell of books. So, when I made making books my profession, I dug in deep on the best ways to print books.

For years, I would try to talk to authors about how to print books in more economical, and more beautiful ways, but my enthusiasm fell flat. Nobody cared. Why would you print and store books if Amazon could just print and deliver books whenever somebody ordered one?

With the recent uptick in interest regarding direct sales, people are finally catching on to all the different ways that producing beautiful books can be a boon to your author business. Besides, it's fun to create something beautiful, especially when you have fans who appreciate the effort.

I've been printing books since before companies like Bookvault and 48 Hour Books significantly expanded what you could do with print-on-demand books, back when the only economical way to create hardcover books was to print 1,000+ copies.

Back then, we basically had Ingramspark, Createspace (RIP), and Lulu, which was a beautiful but ungodly expensive option in those days. If you wanted anything special, or you wanted to print books in color, the only option was to produce an offset run of books.

I see a lot of authors asking questions about printing, and I see a lot of well-meaning authors giving god-awful advice, so I thought I would dump all the information about printing that I've acquired over the last 15 years of printing books. I've asked my friend Lily Wong from Alpaca Color Printing to help me with this task. She's been one of my printer reps since 2015 and helped me print almost all my offset runs.

POD (PRINT-ON-DEMAND) VS. OFFSET PRINTING

POD is printed on smaller machines. If you want to print only a handful of books, or even just one copy, then POD is a fine choice. If you need to print thousands of copies, you should choose offset printing because the more you print the more you save. -Lily Wong

It used to be that the only choices you could make when printing books POD was whether you wanted gloss or matte laminate for our covers (*I always choose matte because the feel is delightful*). There was a time when we couldn't even choose paper weight or anything.

Now, companies like Lulu, Bookvault, Mixam, and 48 Hour Books have a million options from gold foil to glow-in-the-dark and much more. Digital printing used to look cheap, but over the last 15 years we've seen incredible advancements in the quality of POD books.

I should mention here that POD wasn't always around. Before the early 2000s, you couldn't even print digitally. The *only* option was an offset print run.

If you've been in indie publishing for fewer than 10 years, it's likely that you don't even know what offset printing is, which is wild to me since it used to be the only way to print books.

Aside from quality, which I think has vastly improved in the last 3-5 years on the POD side, the main reason to choose offset printing instead of digital printing is cost. While it costs more to do an offset print run, as you have to order a minimum of 250 copies, you save significantly when you start printing at higher volumes.

COST DIFFERENCE IN POD VS. OFFSET PRINTING

Offset printing is printed on a bigger, more complicated machine. They will adjust the color for consistent printing across your entire order. Additionally, when you print more, the cost is less. When you have bigger quantities, like 1,000 copies or above, it saves cost while providing better quality. For offset printing ,100 copies is expensive because each process has a lot of waste. We also need to make CTP plates for the big offset machine. All the waste are divided to each copy. So printing more saves more. - Lily Wong

The biggest argument I have with authors is about long-term thinking vs. short-term term thinking and never is this more apparent than when we talk about print runs.

Why? Offset printing costs more upfront than POD, but it's vastly more cost-effective over the long term. I still have books I printed in 2016 that I'm selling today at no additional cost to me.

Yes, it does take longer-term thinking to plan for the next 3-5 years of your life, but if you know you're going to be selling the same books for a long time, then it might make sense. The independent publishing industry is traditionally built upon "churn and burn," where you put out a book a month until you burn out, but that model is changing. It was never healthy to begin with, but now we're starting to see how toxic that model is and treating our books with the care they deserve.

If we're focused on maximizing our backlist for years instead of churning and burning our books as fast as possible, an offset run makes more sense. As Lily says above, the more you print during an offset run, the more you save.

This is because almost all the cost of printing an offset run is in the first 500 copies. Why is this? Because it costs a lot to create the plates used to print your books. With digital printing, there are no plates, so the cost is consistent, but with offset printing, they create new plates for every job (which is what Lily means above with there being a lot of waste), so you get economy of scale.

Let's talk numbers for a minute. For a digital print run, a paperback copy of *Ichabod Jones: Monster Hunter* costs about $6 to print through Ingramspark. The print quality is pretty good, but it's not perfect. The color is pretty crappy, actually. Still, for a down-and-dirty print job, it's fine.

A few years ago, I printed 1,000 copies of the same book in hardcover, on beautiful paper, with ribbons and everything. That whole run cost about $4,000. So, for

$4/book, I was able to get a higher quality print, on better paper, in hardcover.

That paperback version sells for $20, while the hardcover sells for $30, too. So, yes, if I was printing 100 copies, then it would probably be absurd to print those hardcover books…but that's only if I thought I would never sell those books again.

You see, I still have hundreds of those books in my garage that have been paid off years ago. Every time I did a new volume of Ichabod, I didn't have to print those books again. I already had them. Yes, I had to make that investment upfront, but by printing more I saved more.

And I didn't even print a lot of books. I did the math once, and for every 500 more books I printed, it would have only cost me $750. I found that my best value was around 2,000 books, but that's a lot of books to store at a time. Plus, the more books you have to sell, the fewer books of any one title you seem to sell. I sell roughly the same amount at shows now as I did years ago, but across dozens more books.

UPGRADING YOUR BOOKS ECONOMICALLY

One of the other things that stands out about offset printing is that while it's more expensive to get an initial order, upgrading to better and better options is way more affordable.

For instance, in order to upgrade to hardcover in most POD printers, there is roughly a $4/book upcharge, making hardcover not very economical. Not to mention if you want the binding to be sewn-bound instead of glue-bound. Lily is unequivocal on her preference here.

You need to choose sewn-bound. It is stronger and lays flat. If you do not care about quality, or if you need something like advertising brochures or magazines that are not for long-term use, you can choose glue-bound, not sewn. -Lily Wong

When I went to quote sewn-bound hardcovers from a digital printer, the costs went from $6 to $15, a wild difference, especially since with an offset printer, especially an international printer, it could cost as little as $.83 to upgrade from paperback to sewn-bound hardcover.

That says nothing about the other improvements you can make to books. One day I was trying to find a POD option for spot UV, a process that adds a shine to only certain areas of a cover, and found that you had to pay $5/book for that option on a book, whereas I could get it for $.10 or less from an offset printer.

That's not to say there aren't a ton of options when it comes to digital printing, but offset printing becomes way more economical as you start to create premium and then super premium books, especially the ones I see people offering on Kickstarter.

I should mention that in general, this pricing is only true for overseas printers like Alpaca Printing. Companies like Marquis in Canada or ones in the USA tend to vastly overprice these upgrades, which to me is the most compelling reason to look internationally.

GANG PRINTING, GANG BINDING, AND SPLIT RUNS

You can save money if you print several books together because we can put two covers or three covers on the same plate. If your books are the same size, we can bind them together without the need to adjust the machine. If your book uses the same paper, we can also purchase paper together and save costs. -Lily Wong

Often, authors tell me that they could never sell 1,000+ books. I'm not saying it doesn't take a lot of effort, but there is also an ingenious way to break up your print run to take advantage of several marketing strategies. It is called **gang-binding**, or **split runs**.

The general idea is that you can bind a print run in several different ways to service different markets. For instance, let's say you run a Kickstarter and need 50 leatherbound books, 100 hardcover books, and 200 paperback books.

Well, you might go to a POD printer for that order, or you can go to an offset printer and print them together to take advantage of those economies of scale, and since the interiors are the same, you would really be paying for 350 books with what is called a "change fee" of between $50-$250 per new cover.

Comics are notorious for using this trick to produce dozens of variant covers, including show variants and getting people to rebuy the same book multiple times. Any single book could have 10-20 or more variant covers, all with the same interior paper stock. All they are doing is changing the covers and getting their readers to buy the same book multiple times.

This isn't something that independent authors have taken to as much, but it happens all the time in comics and book publishing and I think we should lean into it. We have:

- Paperback covers
- Mass market covers
- Hardcover
- Limited edition covers
- Book Club covers
- Retailer exclusive covers
- Kickstarter exclusive covers
- Convention covers
- Anniversary covers
- Leather covers

Plus more that I'm probably forgetting, but the point is that if you parcel these covers out then ordering 1,000+ books doesn't seem that bonkers anymore.

If you want to save even more money, then you can order multiple books together, called **gang printing**. This doesn't mean you have to order the books. You could create a little consortium of authors and order 2-5+ books at the same time and save. Maybe consortiums exist for the sole reason of saving on printing costs.

I ordered a book several years ago that cost $10,000 to bring 2,000 copies. When I went to place a second order, I was able to print books 1 and 2 in the series for $12,000, saving me a ton of money. Yes, there are price breaks with POD books, but you're not saving as much as you do with an offset run. ***This is really how you game the publishing system for fun and profit.***

One other thing I want to mention here is that every book size has a different unit of paper they consider their standard measurement. This usually ranges from 12-16 pages and is called a **signature.**

When you print to the signature, meaning you have the exact right page count equal to their unit of measurement, then you save a lot of money. Printing to signature is one of the easiest ways to save money on a print run.

WHEN SHOULD YOU CONSIDER PRINTING LOCALLY, OR POD?

If you print in small quantities, less than 500 copies, it's probably best to print locally. -Lily Wong

I'll be honest. Even though I know all of this, I haven't printed an offset run since 2022. *Why?* Because most of my books are printed in 100-200 unit runs and I have a quick turnaround time.

If you print overseas, you should expect 3-4 months turnaround time. If your order is for a small quantity of paperback books, then people might receive their order in two months. -Lily Wong

The biggest thing that prevents me from printing more books in an offset run, besides space, is that I want to deliver books within a month of a campaign ending, and usually within 2 weeks.

While my longer series could warrant an offset run, printing 12 books is prohibitively expensive, even if I take advantage of all these tricks, especially since people usually only buy 50-100 of any single title during a campaign.

I'm also not offering a lot of filigree or enhancements to my books. They are no-nonsense paperbacks, which is when you see the least value in offset printing. While paperbacks are cheaper when ordered at scale, the delta between them and ordering from a POD printer is nominal compared to hardcover or other enhancements.

WHAT ARE SOME OF THE ENHANCEMENTS I SHOULD CONSIDER FOR MY BOOKS?

Not every printer does every type of enhancement, but these are some of the coolest enhancements I have seen.

Die-cutting means part of the cover is cut out revealing the artwork underneath. If you work in comics, this is an amazing enhancement to your work.

Embossing and debossing allow you to raise or lower parts of the cover so they stand out more from the rest of the book.

UV Spot allows you to add a pop of gloss to make certain parts of your image shine. I prefer matte covers, so I use them all the time. Another one I use all the time is adding a ribbon to my books.

One I am too scared to do is ***sequential numbering*** as it's hard to make sure somebody gets the right number, but it's a popular one.

Glow-in-the-dark is super popular with fans. I only have one cover that glows, and it's generally regarded as people's favorite cover we've ever done.

You can also add ***glitter, gold foil, silver foil,*** or other types of foil to the cover.

You've probably seen a lot of people adding *gilded or painted edges* to their books.

You can also add a *dust jacket*, though I find them more of a pain than a help, as they often tear leading to complaints. I've seen some people do cool things with half or quarter-dust jackets.

If you have a black-and-white book but want to add some color illustrations, you can create an *insert* inside your book that shows off the color images without paying for full color.

You also have some options for cover material, like *cloth or leather,* that can make your books feel special.

Finally, you can create a *slipcase* for your book that protects it in a specially-made box.

I'm sure there are more, but those are the main ones I've seen that work for indie authors.

WHAT ABOUT SHIPPING BOOKS TO ME?

There are five terms you need to know when shipping books internationally.

- **Free On Board (*FOB*)** is a shipment term that defines the point in the supply chain when a buyer or seller becomes liable for the goods being transported. Purchase orders between buyers and sellers specify the FOB terms and help determine ownership, risk, and transportation costs.
- **Cost, Insurance, and Freight (*CIF*)** is an international shipping agreement, which represents the charges paid by a seller to cover the costs, insurance,

and freight of a buyer's order while the cargo is in transit.

- **Delivered Duty Unpaid (*DDU*)** is an international trade term meaning the seller is responsible for ensuring goods arrive safely to a destination; the buyer is responsible for import duties. By contrast, Delivered Duty Paid (DDP) indicates that the seller must cover duties, import clearance, and any taxes.

- **Delivered Duty Paid (*DDP*)** shipping is a type of delivery where the seller takes responsibility for all risk and fees of shipping goods until they reach their destination.

- **EX Works (*EXW*)** is an incoterm whereby the buyer of a shipped product pays for the goods when they are delivered to a specified location. FOB, or Free on Board, instead shifts the responsibility of the goods to the buyer as soon as they are loaded onboard the ship.
  -Investopedia

In general, I always choose DDP, because I know I won't owe any additional costs once the boats cross the ocean. As Lily has told me many times, this is easily the most expensive option. I know that I'm spending a premium, but I just don't want the hassle.

The number of complaints I've heard from friends who were hit with additional charges when they chose FOB or CIP or had to rent a truck to pick the books up at a port is extensive. Unless you know a freight forwarder or would like to learn all about logistics, I highly recommend you bite the bullet and pay more for DDP.

WHAT IF I WANT TO SHIP BOOKS TO A FULFILLMENT COMPANY AND NEVER WANT TO TOUCH THEM?

One of the biggest questions I get asked by authors deals with hassle. They don't want to ship their books or store their books. While you can ship books to a fulfillment company like Merrick Books or Shipbob, there is one big issue with this; *signing the books.*

Luckily, there is a solution for you; tip-in sheets.

A tipped-in page or, if it is an illustration, tipped-in plate, is **a page that is printed separately from the main text of the book, but attached to the book**. A tipped-in page may be glued onto a regular page or even bound along with the other pages. -Wikipedia

When you order tip-ins, the printer sends you a box of paper to sign. Then, you ship them back to the printer and they add them to the book after printing. This is how all big publishers deal with signed books. Brandon Sanderson doesn't get delivered a million books to sign. He gets a million pages to sign and then the printer deals with it.

I want to thank my friend Lily Wong from Alpaca Color Printing. If you want to talk to her about printing your books, then you can email sales@alpacaprinting.com.

The last thing I wanted to do in this section was to provide a glossary of terms you could use for discussion with your printer contacts. These might not be the only terms you need, but they will get you a long way to speaking the same language as your printer.

- **POD** - Print on Demand. It's a printing technology where books or other documents are printed individually as orders come in, rather than in bulk.
- **Offset** - A traditional printing method where ink is transferred from a plate to a rubber blanket and then onto the printing surface.
- **IngramSpark** is a publishing platform that allows authors and publishers to create and distribute print books and ebooks. It's a service provided by Ingram Content Group, one of the largest book distributors in the world. IngramSpark enables users to print on demand, meaning books are printed and shipped when ordered, eliminating the need for large print runs and storage of inventory. It offers various formats, including hardcover, paperback, and ebooks, and distributes to a wide range of retailers and libraries.
- **Amazon KDP (Kindle Direct Publishing)** is Amazon's self-publishing platform. It allows authors to publish their books in digital format (ebooks) and in print through Amazon's print-on-demand service, formerly known as CreateSpace. With KDP, authors can upload their manuscripts, create book covers, set prices, and make their books available for sale on Amazon's various global marketplaces. KDP also provides various promotional tools and analytics to help authors track their sales and performance.
- **Bookvault** - a POD printing company specializing in printing high-end books and providing integrations to direct sales web stores.
- **Lulu** - Lulu Press is a self-publishing platform where authors can create and publish their own books.
- **Mixam** - A printing company that offers various printing services, including book printing.

- **Gang printing** - Printing multiple different projects or copies on the same sheet to optimize paper usage and cost-effectiveness.
- **Gang Binding** - Binding multiple different printed projects together as a batch.
- **Tip-ins** - Additional pages or materials that are inserted into a book after it has been bound.
- **Shipping** - The process of transporting goods (in this case, books) from one place to another.
- **DDP** - Delivered Duty Paid. It refers to a shipping arrangement where the seller is responsible for all costs and risks associated with transporting goods until they reach the buyer.
- **DDU** - Delivered Duty Unpaid. In this shipping arrangement, the buyer is responsible for the import clearance and any applicable taxes or duties upon arrival.
- **FOB** - Free On Board. It indicates the point at which the seller is no longer responsible for shipping costs or liability for the goods being transported.
- **CIP** - Carriage and Insurance Paid. It's a trade term where the seller pays for transportation and insurance to deliver goods to a specified destination.
- **Signature** - A printed sheet folded to become a part of a book with a certain number of pages. Printing a book to signature will save you money.
- **Register** - The accurate alignment of different colors or elements in printing.
- **Change Fee** - A fee incurred for changing the covers on a book at a printer.
- **Alternate covers** - Different cover designs for the same book.

- **Insert** - Additional materials placed inside a book, such as cards, maps, or other supplemental content.
- **Binding** - The process of fastening or securing the pages of a book together.
- **Paperback** - A book with a flexible paper or cardstock cover.
- **Hardcover** - A book with a rigid cover, usually made of cardboard wrapped in cloth, paper, or leather.
- **Board Book** - A book with thick, durable pages made of cardboard, often designed for young children.
- **Trade** - In the publishing industry, it refers to books that are meant for general retail sale, as opposed to specialized or academic books.
- **Case Binding** - A type of bookbinding where the book block is glued to a cover made of thicker material like cardboard.
- **Die-cutting** - A process of cutting paper or cardboard into specific shapes using a die or mold.
- **Embossing** - Creating a raised design or pattern on paper or cardstock.
- **Gloss** - A shiny and reflective finish applied to printed materials.
- **Matte** - A non-reflective, dull finish applied to printed materials.
- **Lamination** - A thin layer of plastic or similar material applied to the surface of printed materials for protection or enhancement.
- **Paper weight** - The thickness and heaviness of paper, often measured in pounds or grams per square meter (GSM).
- **H/T** - Acronym for High-Touch, referring to a personalized or customized approach in printing or customer service.

- **Sew bound** - Binding pages together by sewing them along the spine.
- **Glow-in-the-dark** - Materials or inks that emit visible light after exposure to light.
- **Spot UV** - A coating applied to specific areas of printed material to create a glossy, raised effect.
- **Bleed** - Printing that extends beyond the trim edge of the sheet, allowing for a margin of error in trimming.
- **CMYK** - Acronym for Cyan, Magenta, Yellow, and Key (Black), the four colors used in color printing.
- **DPI** - Dots Per Inch. It measures the resolution of printed images.
- **Foil** - Metallic or colored material applied to printed materials for a decorative or reflective effect.
- **Overrun** - Producing more copies of a printed item than originally ordered.
- **Ream** - A quantity of paper, usually 500 sheets.
- **Saddle stitch** - A binding method where folded sheets are stapled along the fold line to create a booklet.
- **Scoring** - Creating a crease in paper or cardstock to help it fold cleanly.
- **Spine** - The edge of a book where the pages are bound together.
- **Split run** - Printing different versions of a document in the same print run.
- **GSM** - Grams per Square Meter. It measures the weight or density of paper.
- **Proofing** - The process of reviewing and checking a sample print for errors or quality before final printing.
- **Metal** - In printing, it could refer to metallic inks or foils used for decorative purposes in printing.
- **Slipcase** - a protective box used to keep books or special items safe. It's usually made of strong material

like cardboard or wood and helps shield these items from damage, dust, and light. They're often used for collectible books or special editions, adding both protection and a nice look to the collection.

HOW TO SUCCEED AT LIVE EVENTS

If you're like most indie authors, the idea of selling your books in person might feel somewhere between daunting and ridiculous. Why spend hundreds of dollars on a table, stock, gas, travel, and maybe even a hotel room—just to stand behind a plastic table in a loud convention hall hoping someone buys a $20 paperback? It's easy to think, "There's no way this adds up."

But live events are one of the most underutilized, misunderstood, and transformational tools in your author business.

I've built my career behind the booth hand-selling books to people one conversation at a time. For years, I tabled at 20–30 shows annually. I've sold at massive conventions like San Diego Comic-Con and small-town swap meets where I shared space next to someone peddling handmade soaps. I've done library panels, indie bookstore signings, anime cons, horror expos, and book festivals. Every one of them was part of a bigger system that built my fanbase brick by brick.

In a world drowning in digital ads, the authors who show up in person **stand out**. Live events are not just about sales. They're about connection. And connection—real, face-to-face, hand-you-a-book-and-talk-about-it connection—is the secret weapon most authors completely overlook.

THE TOTEM EFFECT

People don't buy books at conventions because they're desperate for something to read. They buy them because the book becomes a physical artifact of an experience. A souvenir.

That's the magic. You're not just selling a story. You're selling a moment, and moments are priceless.

At shows, people spend money more freely than they do online. Why? Because they're in buying mode. They've paid to attend. They've set aside time. They're looking for something cool to discover. When you offer a beautiful book with a compelling pitch and an enthusiastic attitude, it becomes that something.

Doing shows is also a great way to stand out. **You're not one author out of millions anymore**. You're one of maybe a dozen at a specific event. You went from being a pixel in someone's feed to a real person, standing behind a table, smiling and talking about your work.

That's not just visibility. That's memorability.

We live in a world of noise. Scrolling. Ads. Email blasts. Everyone wants attention, but no one wants to build trust. And trust is what drives sales, not just today, but six months from now.

At a show, when someone stops at your table and chats, even if they don't buy, they've had a touchpoint with your brand. If they sign up for your mailing list or take a bookmark, that's another. If they see you again at another show and remember you, that's another. Touchpoint. Touchpoint. Touchpoint. Eventually, that person becomes a fan.

Here's something most authors don't realize: your job isn't just to sell. It's to be remembered.

Maybe they won't buy today. Maybe they'll go home and Google you. Maybe they'll buy your book next year on Kickstarter. Or sign up for your Substack. Or tell a friend.

That's the long game. And live events are the best way to play it.

CONVERTING AT THE SPEED OF TRUST

Digital selling is a slow burn. You run ads, people click, maybe they browse your page, maybe they bounce. Maybe you get lucky. Maybe you don't.

In-person sales are different. They're visceral. You hand someone a book. You pitch. You ask questions. You joke. You connect. **It's all trust-building in real time.**

And trust converts.

When someone sees your passion, hears your story, and senses your excitement, it short-circuits the usual skepticism that comes with buying from an unknown author. They might not have planned to buy a book today, but something about the experience makes them say yes.

That yes didn't come from a 3-step email funnel or a perfectly optimized product page. It came from **you**.

BUILDING MOMENTUM

It's important to understand that live events aren't just about what you make at the table. They're about momentum. Here's what I mean:

- You meet vendors and forge partnerships.
- You network with panelists and get invited to future events.
- You speak on stage, which opens doors to even more credibility.
- You gather hundreds of emails for your list.
- You test new pitches, price points, and product bundles.

Even at a "bad" show, I walk away with something valuable. A new friend. A contact. A lesson. A photo of my booth I can post to build social proof. Every single one of those things feeds my business.

There are thousands of authors with beautiful books and optimized ads and stunning websites. But very few of them show up.

If you want to be remembered, if you want people to talk about your work, if you want to accelerate your growth instead of inching forward, you have to get in front of real people.

Will it be exhausting? Yes. Will it sometimes feel thankless? Yes. Will it be worth it? Absolutely.

Live events have made me more money, built me deeper relationships, and opened more doors than any single marketing tactic I've ever used.

And I want the same for you.

CHOOSING THE RIGHT SHOWS (AND SETTING EXPECTATIONS)

Not all events are created equal. Some conventions are well-oiled machines with tens of thousands of attendees and years of brand equity. Others are held in hotel ballrooms with a few hundred people and a shaky Facebook page. So how do you know which ones are worth your time?

The truth is, you won't always know. There's a lot of trial and error in the live events game. But that doesn't mean you have to walk in blind.

KNOW YOUR PURPOSE

Before you book a table, it's important to align your goals and expectations. What are you there to do?

- **Make money?** You'll want high-foot-traffic shows with a strong buying culture.
- **Build your mailing list?** Target smaller, community-driven events where conversations flow more easily.
- **Network with other creators or vendors?** Look for multi-day shows with artist alleys or robust programming.
- **Gain exposure and speak?** Consider conferences or festivals that allow panel submissions.

Most shows won't serve all these goals. And that's okay. But knowing your *primary objective* keeps you from misjudging the value of a weekend. You might not make $1,000 in sales, but if you meet two future collaborators and add 150 people to your list, that might be a win.

TYPES OF EVENTS

Let's break this down by category:

- **Conventions (Comic, Anime, Horror, etc.):** Big crowds, mixed interests. Great for genre authors. Expect competition.
- **Book Festivals:** Often reader-focused, with panels, readings, and signings. Ideal for literary, memoir, and genre fiction.
- **Writers Conferences:** Fantastic for networking, but harder for direct sales. These are more about industry connections and craft.
- **Farmer's Markets & Local Fairs:** Cheap tables, friendly crowds. A good training ground for new sellers.
- **Store Signings & Library Events:** Lower foot traffic, but higher engagement. Good for building local community presence.
- **Signing events:** There are lots of genre specific book signing events now that cater to readers, like RARE and BABE.

Don't let size seduce you. A 50,000-person convention can result in $300 in sales. A 1,000-person boutique con might net $3,000. It's all about audience fit and your ability to convert.

Small events also let you test pitches, merchandise setups, and new books with lower stakes. They're great laboratories. Don't discount them.

HOW TO FIND THE RIGHT EVENTS

- **Facebook groups and Reddit threads** about local shows or niche genres.

- **ConventionScene.com** and similar databases.
- **Bookstores and libraries**, who often know about local literary events.
- **Asking fellow authors** where they've had success.

For a sales-based event, your goal should be to **10X your table cost** or **2X your total show expenses (including travel)**. That's not always realistic at first, but setting that bar will help you analyze ROI accurately.

If a table is $200, you're aiming for $2,000 in gross sales. If you spent $1,000 getting to and working the show, you want to bring in $2,000 to justify it.

Track this. Every time.

PREPARING FOR THE CONVENTION FLOOR

You've booked your table. You've shipped your books. Now what?

Now it's time to think like a stage designer. Because at live events, your table is your storefront, your resume, and your personality, all wrapped in six feet of folding real estate.

Long before you say a word, your booth is doing the talking. Does it look inviting? Does it scream "this is worth checking out?" Or does it look like someone dumped a box of books and bounced?

Here's what you need:

- **A clean, table drape** (bring your own—it's worth it).
- **A branded runner or banner** that showcases your name or series.
- **Verticality by** using shelves, risers, or wire stands to show off covers at eye level.

- **Freebies** like bookmarks that act as icebreakers.
- **A mailing list signup mechanism**—clipboard, tablet, QR code, whatever works.
- **Filigree is not my favorite thing,** but there's no doubt if you bring some sort of twinkle lights or confetti it will catch a reader's eye.

If you're more introverted, great design can sell books without you saying much. If you're extroverted, great design makes your pitch easier.

WHAT TO BRING

- Copies of your books (obvi; double copies of book one in any series)
- Business cards or bookmarks
- Credit card reader (Square, PayPal, etc.)
- Cash box and change
- Tape, pens, scissors, clips—your author tool kit
- Water, snacks, comfortable shoes

MERCH: THE UPSELL GAME

Books might be your main product, but merch can sweeten deals and improve margins:

- Pins, buttons, stickers, and prints add personality and profit.
- Bundle items for deals like: "Buy 2 books, get a pin free."
- Use merch as mailing list incentives or buyer bonuses.

Think in bundles. You want the average sale to be $40. That's the magic number. A $20 book and a $20 add-on. Or 3 paperbacks for $40. That adds up quickly, and if you price your bundles at $50, you just two sales an hour hits $100/hr.

PITCHING AND CLOSING WITH CONFIDENCE

Let's get something clear right away: pitching isn't about being pushy. It's about having a conversation. It's about inviting someone into your world and helping them decide whether or not they want to stay.

A good pitch doesn't feel like a pitch. It feels like a chat with someone who genuinely cares about whether this book is right for them. So let's talk about how to make that happen.

- Stand up. Smile. Be approachable.
- Ask questions: "Are you a reader?" "What's your favorite genre?"
- Use bookmarks to draw people in.
- Offer a confident, quick pitch: "This series is Buffy meets Star Wars with a splash of Lovecraft."
- Use the "optional close": "Do you prefer dark fantasy or sci-fi?" instead of "Do you want to buy my book?"

Remember: your job isn't to *convince*, it's to *connect*. Let your excitement be contagious.

THE BOOKMARK TRICK

One of my favorite ways to start a conversation is with a simple question:

"Would you like a free bookmark?"

It's low-pressure. Friendly. A natural lead-in. And while they're reaching for it, you follow up with:

"Have you heard of my books before?"

Boom, you're in a conversation. From there, you can start the pitch. This is a really low lift way for introverts and quiet authors to succeed.

THE QUESTION FUNNEL

This is where sales psychology comes into play. You want to guide the customer using **closed-ended questions** that help you understand their preferences:

"Do you like fantasy or sci-fi?"

"Do you like psychological thrillers or action-packed stories?"

"Are you into dark humor or hopeful tales?"

Each question helps you tailor your pitch. And every time they answer, they're saying a little "yes"—a micro-commitment that makes it easier for them to say a big "yes" when you ask if they want to buy.

THE OPTIONAL CLOSE

Instead of asking, "Do you want to buy this book?" try:

"Would you like book one, or would you like the bundle with the pin and print?"

Or:

"Do you want to grab just this one, or complete the trilogy?"

You're assuming the sale—but offering options. It works because you're never forcing. You're just guiding.

MY 6-STEP PITCH FORMULA

This process is designed to move a customer from zero interest to a confirmed sale in under a minute. Here are the steps with commentary and actionable framing:

STEP 1: THE QUESTION

Open with a **simple yes/no** or **binary choice** question that filters for interest:

- "Do you like murder mysteries?"
- "Looking for something to make your kid fall asleep?"
- "Are you more into fantasy or sci-fi?"

This gets people engaged and self-identifying as part of your target market. Each "yes" builds momentum.

STEP 2: THE OPTION

Present two specific options tied to your inventory:

- "Do you prefer killer women or psychological thrillers?"
- "Do you like cute monsters or scary ones?"

This narrows their focus and makes the conversation more personal while guiding you to the right pitch track.

STEP 3: THE PITCH

Now that they've engaged and made a choice, deliver a **tight, emotionally resonant hook**:

- "This book is *Buffy the Vampire Slayer* meets *Lovecraft*—a cosmic horror adventure with a badass heroine."

Focus on:

- Emotion over plot.
- Comps over deep dives.
- Benefits over features.

Keep it under 30 seconds.

STEP 4: THE FLAVOR

Once they're holding the book or glancing at the cover, add unique value:

- "The artist on this went on to draw *Star Wars*."
- "Every book comes with a sketch card inside."

You're adding spice by dropping in little, compelling details that enhance their experience and justify the purchase.

STEP 5: THE ACCEPTANCE

Before closing, ask for one more micro-yes:

- "Pretty cool, right?"
- "That sounds like your kind of story?"

It primes them emotionally. It's low-pressure but nudges them toward commitment.

STEP 6: THE ASK

Now go in for the sale:

- "Would you like just this one, or the set with the bonus pin?"
- "Do you want to grab a signed copy or unsigned?"

Use the **optional close**: offer a binary choice, not yes/no. Assume the sale. Let them decide how, not if.

TIPS FOR GREAT PITCHES

- **Keep it short.** 20–30 seconds max before you let somebody else talk. Think movie trailer, not TED Talk.
- **Use comps.** "It's like Stranger Things meets Narnia." That shortcut makes a huge difference.
- **Match their energy.** If they're quiet, don't go full carnival barker. If they're excited, match that vibe.
- **Don't overwhelm.** Too many books on the table? Focus their attention. Pick one and talk about that.
- **Have a fallback.** If they're not into your main book, be ready to pivot: "If you like thrillers, I also have this…"

Remember: every pitch is a conversation. And every conversation is a chance to connect.

THE LONG GAME OF CONVENTION SELLING

Conventions are not just for this weekend. They're for the next decade of your career.

There are thousands of authors online. Most of them are invisible. But when you show up at the same event two years in a row? You become a familiar face. Familiarity builds trust. Trust builds sales.

I can't tell you how many people have said, "I saw you at [event] last year!" and then bought something this time. Sometimes they just weren't ready before. Now they are.

Showing up is half the job. Showing up *again* is what makes you a fixture.

Every show you do builds your email list. Every person you meet could become a backer, a reader, a fan. Maybe they won't buy today. But if they're on your list, you can reach them tomorrow.

It's a flywheel. And the more you turn it, the faster it spins.

You also build relationships with vendors, organizers, and other creators. That leads to:

- Panel invites
- Speaking gigs
- Cross-promotions
- Co-author opportunities

Each show becomes a stepping stone to the next. A long runway to success.

You're not just selling books. You're building a creative ecosystem. A world of stories, merchandise, mailing lists, fan communities, panels, and brand recognition.

And live events are the anchor.

Don't worry if you don't make five figures at your first con. Worry about getting better. Worry about being memorable. Worry about collecting emails. Worry about giving people a moment they'll remember.

If you do that, the money will come.

WHAT'S NEXT?

It's over!

If you've read this far, I want to thank you for your persistence and perseverance. I know that learning about business isn't any creator's favorite thing to do in the world; however, just by reading this book, you are so much further ahead than most creatives on this planet.

I would say to give yourself a round of applause, but I've worked very hard throughout this book not to be cheesy and don't want to ruin it now.

Well, maybe just a little applause would be okay. Not too long, though, because now the real work begins.

That's right…work.

As much knowledge as I crammed into this book, it's truly just a primer to gear you up for a lifelong pursuit of learning about the business of art. The goal of this book is to give you the necessary tools so you can go out there and build the foundation of a creative career.

It's not an endpoint. It's a beginning.

You made it to the end of this book. Now, you are prepared for the horrible and yet consistent world of late-stage capitalism. However, you still have to live in it.

If you loved this book, I hope you go check out *The Author Stack,* my weekly newsletter that goes into even more depth about how to build your creator career.

https://www.theauthorstack.com/

As a paid member, you get access to a ton of my previous work, including fiction, non-fiction, courses, and more.

RESOURCES:

- *How to Build Your Creative Career*
- *How to Become a Successful Author*
- *Advanced Growth Tactics for Authors*
- Create Profitable Facebook Ads course
- Fund Your Book with Kickstarter course
- How to set up and run an awesome anthology course
- How to run a viral giveaway to build your mailing list
- Write a Great Novel course
- How to Build an Audience from Scratch minicourse
- 10x your productivity course
- Lessons and lectures
- Interview archive
- Complete Creative data archive
- Income reports since 2018
- Script library

There's probably even more now since I update it every couple of months.

You can also find my work at: www.russellnohelty.com

Feel free to email me at russell@wannabepress.com and let me know what you think, and please leave a review. The only way I know I should keep writing these kinds of books is from your reviews and kind words.

Find more of my work at my blog:

www.theauthorstack.com

Find all my work at my website:

www.russellnohelty.com

Bookbub:

https://www.bookbub.com/profile/russell-nohelty

www.ingramcontent.com/pod-product-compliance
Lightning Source LLC
Chambersburg PA
CBHW070103030426
42335CB00016B/1995